First Edition 2011

I0102437

We Are

The Majority

Scott Beebe

Losus Media, Inc.

WeAreTheMajority.net

We Are The Majority
Scott Beebe

Publisher: Createspace, part of the Amazon group of companies

Cover: Designed and created by Brian Beebe, www.brian-beebe.com

Printed and bound in the United States of America.

ISBN-10: 061557405X

ISBN-13: 978-0615574059

Pending registration with the Library of Congress

We Are The Majority

We Are The Majority

Table of Contents

Acknowledgements

Special thanks to my wonderful wife whose unflagging support and help are invaluable. Her enthusiasm made this book possible.

Thanks to my son, Brian, for the artwork and computer support.

And heartfelt thanks to the readers who slogged through the manuscripts, giving insightful and valuable help in shaping this book.

Acknowledgements

Preface

The seed for *We Are The Majority* germinated when the Healthcare Reform Act came up for a vote. The polls were consistent and conclusive: the majority of Americans were against the bill. It passed anyway.

The government continued to pass bills we disagreed with or defeated bills we did agree with. Government spending continued unabated and deficits soared. The polls continued to reflect a growing disillusionment and disgust with our leaders. I soon discovered that most people I knew felt like I did: the government went against our beliefs, values, and judgment.

Then I heard about a poll stating that a large majority of Americans believe the government rules without the consent of the governed. So I started to investigate the polls to discover who is the majority voice in America. The results are in these pages.

We live in America, and that means we the people have the power to transform our government if the majority of the people unite together. But we must vote, and vote for those who truly represent our beliefs and values.

I hope this book aids that transformation.

Chapter 1

Who Is The Majority?

"...That to secure the Rights, Governments are instituted among
   men, deriving their just Powers from the Consent of the
   Governed..."

Declaration of Independence

Only 17% of Americans believe our government has the consent
   of the governed.[1]

Rasmussen poll dated 8/7/2011

Something is terribly wrong. The Great Experiment of rule by the people, for the people, is crumbling around us: 83% of Americans believe that our government ignores the founding principle of our country.[1] That's huge. And hugely sad. How do we have a representative government that does not represent us? Who is this majority?

The best source to determine the majority is NOT the media, the politicians, or academia; it is the extensive polls conducted by Rasmussen, Gallup, Zogby, and Pew Research. By cutting through the spin and going right to the American people, we can identify the unrepresented majority.

Will it be a completely unified voice? Of course not. Americans are independent thinkers with our individual ideas, values, and beliefs. However, an American majority does exist and the upcoming elections are the opportunity to re-instate the principle of the consent of the governed.

Polling Data

The conclusions of this book are based upon the polling data. The accuracy of opinion polls is often viewed with skepticism. We tend to respond emotionally to polling results, believing the data is scientifically accurate when we agree with the results and disregarding the data when we disagree with the results. You will not find that type of flip-flopping in this book. The polls are the polls. No attempt is made to spin the polls or to explain away the results.

The scientific accuracy of public opinion polling remains elusive. The accuracy of election polls is easy to determine once the election is complete, but public opinion polls have no conclusive, empirical measurement to verify the results. We know that the participants and the way the questions are phrased can influence the findings. The polling companies must present an impartial and balanced question to a true representative sample. For that reason, only polls from the major polling companies are included in this book.

Even so, we can be left with the nagging feeling that public opinion polls aren't scientific. In fact, our politicians often dispute polling results when the polls do not agree with them. However, Wharton professor of statistics J. Michael Steele says:

> "Surveys conducted by professional polling organizations on a periodic basis which repeatedly ask the same question...are fully scientific and useful."[2]

J. Michael Steele

Thisnation.com is even more straight-forward:

> "Believe it or not, when conducted properly, public opinion polling is generally quite accurate."[3]

When properly conducted, the consensus is that public opinion polls are reliable. The professional organizations of Rasmussen, Gallup, Zogby, and Pew Research are used by, and quoted by, the media, the politicians, and any and everyone who uses polls to make a point or gather public support. As the accepted standard of the industry, these polls are believed to yield results that accurately reflect the opinion of the American people. And in America, the opinion of the people is supposed to translate into the power of the people.

Power of the People

The power of the people is what makes America great. With the collapse of the Soviet Union in the 1980s, we are the world's only superpower. Why? Are we a special people? The idea that Americans are superior is not politically correct, nor is it entirely accurate. Perhaps we are not any smarter, harder working, or in any way superior to the rest of the world. So if the people in America are the same as people anywhere, why is America so successful?

If we listen to the media, it's because Americans are greedy, grasping, diabolical human beings bent on destroying anyone and anything as we rape the world of its wealth and resources. That sounds like you and your neighbors, right? Some say it's luck. We have excellent land, ample water, and extensive natural gas, oil, and coal reserves. That is lucky. However, luck alone cannot create a prosperous society.

It is the attitude and sweat of our citizens that creates a prosperous society. Americans forged a powerful and prosperous nation because we are free to enjoy the fruits of our labor. Our system of government stresses individual rights and personal accomplishment, and allows us to strive for all the success that our abilities and motivation can obtain. Our Founding Fathers gave us a government of limited powers that allows us to live free, pursue dreams, and share in the wealth of the nation.

Our Founders had a remarkable vision. This is not to say they were perfect or that the Constitution was perfect, but the ideals and wisdom of our Founders created the fairest, greatest rule of law under which an individual could thrive. Americans live the promises originated in the Declaration of Independence:

> "...that they (men) are endowed, by their Creator, with certain unalienable Rights, that among these are Life, Liberty, and the Pursuit of Happiness..."
>
> *Declaration of Independence*

This single statement resulted in a republic where the people created great wealth and power; a republic where the power of the people is to be represented in our government.

America is a Republic

It is important to note that the form of government in the United States is a republic, not a democracy. The Constitution declares:

> "The United States shall guarantee to every State in this Union a Republican Form of Government."
>
> *United States Constitution*

For years, we all said the Pledge of Allegiance:

> I pledge allegiance to the flag of the United States of America, and to the *republic* for which it stands, one nation under God, indivisible, with liberty and justice for all.

Yet, if asked what type of government we live under, most will answer a democracy. Even *Merriam-Webster.com* lists democracy as a synonym for republic. 200 years ago, the terms were not synonymous.

Republic and Democracy

It is easy to confuse democratic elections with democracy:

- Democratic elections: where the people vote and the majority vote wins. The vote can be for legislation, representatives, taxes, and so on, but the vote is directly by the citizens.

- Democracy: where the people decide matters of policy by direct means, either town hall meetings or by voting on ballot initiatives and referendums through democratic elections.[4]

While a democracy definitely gives power to the people, it is an impractical method of governing and a recipe for tyranny by the majority.

By definition, a democracy means our citizens would vote on every expenditure by the federal, state, and local governments from health care reform to paving roads to permits to creating financial regulations and on and on. We'd be full-time voters! Not very practical.

Democracy also becomes tyranny because the majority vote always wins. That doesn't sound bad but what if the majority is self-serving and strips the unalienable rights of a law-abiding citizen? Such was the concern of our Founding Fathers:

> "....that such democracies...have ever been found incompatible with personal security or the rights of property..."[5]
>
> *James Madison*

Having stated that man is endowed by God with unalienable rights, our Founders were seeking a system of government that prevented the rulers, or the mob, from supplanting the rights of the citizens. Instead, they created a representative system whose power resides in the people, but is constrained by the checks and balances of the Constitution. That system is our republic.

> Republic: A political order in which the supreme power lies in a body of citizens who are entitled to vote for officers and representatives responsible to them.[6]

The citizens vote for local, state, and federal government representatives in democratic elections. We expect our representatives to act in the best interest of their voters, to generally align themselves with the will of their voters, and to thoughtfully and prudently exam all issues. We do not expect our representatives to vote on 2,000 page bills they did not read.

In a republic, the voter's job is to vote for the candidate whose values and beliefs represent their own. The representative's job is to govern with integrity and the will to stand up for the shared beliefs. They are to provide a service, a public service, and not be strictly motivated by power and wealth.

You're probably laughing right now. Such candidates do not exist. Yet our history is full of representatives who took the duty of the public trust seriously and considered it a privilege to give years of their lives in public service. Sadly, today politicians are often disdained. Sadder still, many have earned our disdain.

Our republic is designed to represent the majority while preventing the majority from becoming tyrannical. However, if the minority consistently rules over the majority then tyranny is also established. Today, a 17% minority is ruling the 83% majority. It is time for the majority to be represented. But who is the majority?

Chapter 2

Party and Ideology

"The electors are to be the great body of the people of the United States."[1]

James Madison

Our political affiliation and position on the issues is constantly fluctuating, a tribute to our freedom, independence, and right of free-speech. For example, the current majority view that increasing domestic energy production is more important than environmental concerns is a recent development signaling a large shift in the thinking of the citizens (see Chapter 5). However, in general, basic political affiliation and our position on the issues have small fluctuations. Conservatives tend to stay conservative; Liberals tend to stay liberal; and Moderates tend to vacillate between the two.

There are two ways to discover the American majority by using polling data:

- How Americans label themselves

- Where Americans stand on the issues

We shall see if these two methods produce identical results. This chapter will define the labels we use and detail how we apply them, then we will begin looking at the issues.

The Labels

We label ourselves using two separate categories: political party and ideology. On the party side, we have Democrat, Republican, and Independent (or lack of party affiliation). On the ideology side, we have Conservative, Moderate, and Liberal. And no, all Republicans are not Conservative and all Liberals are not Democrats. If only it were so clear!

Political Parties

America is basically a two-party country, Republicans and Democrats.[*] However, a sizable portion of the electorate (citizens who vote) refuses to affiliate with either party. These are the Independents. Webster's Dictionary defines these affiliations as:

> Republican: 1: one that favors or supports a republican form of government. 2: a member of a political party advocating republicanism; a member of the Republican Party of the U.S.[2]

> Democrat: 1: an adherent of democracy; one who practices social equality. 2: a member of the Democratic Party of the U.S.[2]

> Independent:...3: not bound by or committed to a political party...[2]

You chose a political party when you first registered to vote. I registered at my high school, not having the slightest idea of what I was doing or the ideals of my chosen political party. I had no concept of the importance and responsibility of being a voter. This quote from Samuel Adams was never discussed in the classroom:

> "Let each citizen remember at the moment he is offering his vote that he is...executing one of the most solemn trusts in human society for which he is accountable to God and his country."[3]

Samuel Adams

Samuel Adams is almost reverent about voting, an attitude we do not display as barely half of us voted in the last presidential election.[4] Voter turnout aside, we choose to affiliate ourselves with a political party or as an Independent. According to a October, 2011 poll by Rasmussen, the electorate breaks down as follows:[5]

> Republican: 34.3%

> Democrat: 33.1%

> Independent: 32.6%

---

[*]. My apologies to the Libertarian Party: none of the major polling companies provided or asked for information regarding Libertarians in any of the polls I studied. At 4% of the voting population, the number of Libertarians is very small.

This has changed only slightly since 2004:[5]

> Republican: 34.7%
>
> Democrat: 37.4%
>
> Independent: 27.9%

One interpretation of the slight shift in numbers is that some Democrats have left their party and become Independents. But, for the most part, the party affiliation of the electorate has changed little in the last 7 years. This is very interesting when compared to the vast change in the outlook and policies of the Federal government during those same 7 years.

The largest segment of our population is affiliated with Republicans, however, the poll reveals we are virtually split 3 ways as to party affiliation. Therefore, for either party to gain a majority of the vote, assuming most Republicans vote for Republicans and most Democrats vote for Democrats, the Independent vote creates the winning majority. To examine how Independents vote we must study both ideology and issues, as Independents tend to vote on those parameters and not by the party affiliation of the candidate.

For a moment we are going to push aside the political labels and discuss the ideological labels: Conservative, Moderate, and Liberal. After this discussion, we will combine the labels and review the results.

Ideology

Americans are a free-thinking people and we live under a Constitution that promotes free expression. In politics, we use the labels Conservative, Moderate, and Liberal to group together individuals with similar ideas, beliefs, and values. First, let's define these terms starting with Liberal:

> Liberalism: "a political philosophy based on belief in progress, the essential goodness of man, and the autonomy of the individual and standing for the protection of political and civil liberties."[2]
>
> Liberals: "believe in government action to achieve equal opportunity and equality for all. It is the duty of the government to alleviate social ills and to protect civil liberties and individual and human rights. They believe the role of the government should be to guarantee that no one is in need.

Liberal policies generally emphasize the need for the government to solve problems."[6]

"Liberals usually embrace freedom of choice in personal matters, but tend to support significant government control of the economy. They generally support a government-funded "safety net" to help the disadvantaged, and advocate strict regulation of business. Liberals tend to favor environmental regulations, defend civil liberties and free expression, support government action to promote equality, and tolerate diverse lifestyles."[7]

Liberals often see government as the solution.

Next, Conservative:

Conservatism: "disposition in politics to preserve what is established; a political philosophy based on tradition and social stability, stressing established institutions, and preferring gradual development to abrupt change."[2]

Conservatives: "believe in personal responsibility, limited government, free markets, individual liberty, traditional American values and a strong national defense. They believe the role of government should be to provide people the freedom necessary to pursue their own goals. Conservative policies generally emphasize empowerment of the individual to solve problems."[6]

"Conservatives tend to favor economic freedom, but frequently support laws to restrict personal behavior that violates "traditional values." They oppose excessive government control of business, while endorsing government action to defend morality and the traditional family structure. Conservatives usually support a strong military, oppose bureaucracy and high taxes, favor a free-market economy, and endorse strong law enforcement."[7]

Conservatives often see government as the problem.

Typically, Liberals and Conservatives are very consistent in their viewpoint and values. They possess a firm core of beliefs and rarely stray from them when taking a stance on an issue. They have one way of seeing the world and they stick with it. When a Conservative and a Liberal engage in discussions or debates, they often agree on the problem but rarely on the solution.

Conservative vs. Liberal Ideology

A thorough discussion of Conservative and Liberal ideology is outside the scope of this book. Here, we are concerned with who we are and why 83% of us say the government does not represent us. However, to accurately establish this, we need to briefly review the contrasting ideologies to eventually determine which ideology is reflected by the majority. This review will focus on the political issues and the values that have become political issues.

The following table is a merging of information from *balancedpolitics.org,*[8] *studentnewsdaily.com,*[6] and personal observations. Keep in mind that not all Liberals and not all Conservatives will agree with all the items listed here. Generally speaking, this is intended to give a good political sketch of the opposing viewpoints.

These topics are listed alphabetically and do not represent an order of importance to either Conservatives or Liberals:

Topic	Liberal	Conservative
Abortion	Pro-Choice: A woman has the right to decide what happens with her body. A fetus is not a human life and does not have individual rights. Abortion is a personal choice and this right should be protected by the government. The government should pay for abortions for women who cannot afford them.	Pro-Life: Human life begins at conception and a fetus has individual rights like other citizens. Since killing a fetus is murder, the woman does not have the right to an abortion. The government should not pay for abortions, nor protect those who have or perform abortions.

Topic	Liberal	Conservative
Affirmative Action	For: Minorities were deprived of equal education and employment opportunities in the past. The government must make up for that. America is still racist and affirmative action laws are required.	Against: Individuals should be admitted to college or hired for jobs based on their ability, not race. It is unfair to use race as a factor in the selection process. Some Americans are racist, but our society as a whole is not. Affirmative action is racist.
Business	Control: Increase regulation in all aspects of business operation and provide for worker protection.	Free Market: Decrease regulations to promote business and keep government out of business operations.
Crime	Protect the rights of the accused first and foremost.	Protect the rights of the victim first and foremost.
Death Penalty	Ban: Inhumane and 'cruel and unusual' punishment. Imprisonment is appropriate for a murder conviction. Every execution risks killing an innocent person.	Maintain: The death penalty fits the crime of murder, being neither 'cruel' nor 'unusual.' Execution is appropriate for the taking of an innocent life.
Defense Spending	Decrease or maintain: The way to achieve peace in the world is through diplomacy, negotiation, and compromise from a position of working together. Carrot only.	Increase: The way to achieve peace in the world is to engage in diplomacy and negotiation from a position of superior military power. Carrot and stick.

Topic	Liberal	Conservative
Economy	Regulated: Government must protect citizens from the greed of business owners. Government is motivated by public interest. Regulation is needed in all areas of the economy so all Americans can succeed.	Free market: Competitive capitalism and private enterprise create the greatest opportunity and the highest standard of living for all citizens. Free markets produce more economic growth, more jobs, and more income for citizens than government regulated economies.
Education school vouchers	Public schools are the best way to educate students. Vouchers take money away from public schools. Government should raise funding for public schools, teacher salaries, and reduce class size.	School vouchers create competition and therefore encourage schools to improve performance. Vouchers will give all parents the ability to choose good schools for their children, not just those who can afford private schools.
Energy	The government must implement a national plan for all energy resources and subsidize alternative energy research and production. Government control of oil, gas, and electric industries. More conservation, less production.	Increase domestic production of oil, gas, and coal to lower energy prices. Decrease dependence on foreign sources of oil. Support increased use of nuclear energy, while supporting research in viable alternative energy sources. Private ownership of oil, gas, and electric industries.

Topic	Liberal	Conservative
Global Warming/ Climate Change	Global warming is real and caused by fossil fuel emissions. The U.S. is a major contributor because it produces 25% of the world's carbon dioxide. Regulations to reduce carbon emissions are urgently needed to save the planet.	Global warming may be real, but is a natural cycle and is not caused by carbon emissions of human origin. Regulations will not effect global warming and will cause significantly higher energy costs for all citizens, lowering living standards and economic output.
Gun Control	Ban: The Second Amendment does not give citizens the right to keep and bear arms. It is the role of government to protect the people and citizens do not need guns. Gun control will limit the ability of criminals to obtain guns. More guns mean more violence.	Protect: The Second Amendment gives citizens the right to keep and bear arms. Gun control laws do not lower crime rates with guns involved. Better enforcement of existing laws is needed. More guns in the hands of law-abiding citizens means less crime.
Health Care	Socialized Medicine: Every American has a right to affordable health care and millions of Americans are deprived of this basic right. The government should provide equal health care benefits for all.	Free market: Health care should remain privatized. Socialized medicine results in higher costs and reduced quality. The problem of uninsured individuals should be addressed and solved within the free market health care system.

Topic	Liberal	Conservative
Homeland Security- Airports	Passenger profiling is wrong, discriminatory, and offensive to Arabs and Muslims. Terrorists don't fit a profile.	Submitting all passengers to invasive search (whether electronic or physical) is not effective and infringes on individual rights. Profiling and intelligence data should be used to single out passengers for extra screening. Most terrorists do fit a profile.
Illegal Immigration	Grant amnesty to illegal aliens. Illegal aliens have the same rights as American citizens. Do not build a fence along the Mexican border. Prevent a national ID card.	Prevent amnesty to illegal aliens. Illegal aliens do not have the same rights as American citizens. Build a fence along the Mexican border. Create a national ID card. Prosecute employers who hire illegal aliens. Increase *legal* immigration.
Personal Responsibility	Government needs to protect the people from themselves.	People are responsible and need to be held accountable for their actions.
Private Property	Government has the right to use eminent domain to seize private property to accomplish a public end.	Respect ownership and private property rights. The seizure of private property is wrong.

Topic	Liberal	Conservative
Religion and Government	Support the separation of church and state as implied by the Bill of Rights. All references to God in public and government spaces should be removed. Support faith-based government initiatives (see chapter 5).	The phrase "separation of church and state" is not in the Constitution; that Congress cannot establish a national religion is. However, this does not prohibit God from being acknowledged in public and government spaces. Support faith-based government initiatives (see chapter 5).
Social Security	Social security provides a safety net for the nation's poor. Changing the system would cause a reduction in benefits and many people would suffer. Raise Social Security taxes.	Social Security is in financial trouble and major changes are required to prevent the collapse of the system and the suffering of many people. Privatize the system to allow citizens to control their own money.
Taxes	Higher taxes and a larger government are necessary to address inequality and injustice. Government programs are a caring way to provide for the poor and requires high taxes, especially on the rich.	Lower taxes and smaller government will raise the standard of living for all citizens. Money is best spent by those who earn it and not the government. Government programs promote laziness and dependency, not industry and independence.
Terrorism	Terrorism is the result of arrogant U.S. foreign policy. Captured terrorists should be handled by law enforcement and tried in civilian courts with all the rights of Americans.	Terrorism is the result of the religious and political attitudes of militant Islamists. Captured terrorists should be treated as enemy combatants and tried in military courts.

Topic	Liberal	Conservative
Welfare	Welfare is a safety net for the poor and is necessary to bring fairness to American economic life.	Welfare should be temporarily used to help the poor become self-reliant, not dependent on government.

Table 1: Opposing viewpoints of Conservatives and Liberals

Although this is not a comprehensive list, it provides a good snapshot of the opposing viewpoints of Conservatives and Liberals.[*] Such opposing viewpoints should act as an ideological check-and-balance system for our government. Has it worked out that way?

Moderates and Independents

Conservatives and Liberals are much easier to define than Moderates. Conservatives follow conservative views; Liberals follow liberal views; Moderates follow both views simultaneously. How do you define that? We do have a dictionary definition:

> Moderate: A person who is moderate in opinion or opposed to extreme views and actions, especially in politics or religion. A member of a political party advocating moderate reform.[9]

The wording "extreme views" must give us pause. The very definition as quoted here is making a valuation statement on the views of others. We use moderate to mean 'more reasonable,' as if Liberals and Conservatives are by definition unreasonable. (Ask one, see what they think!) As an ideology, moderate is not a statement of 'being reasonable' but a label for a political outlook.

Moderates hold a mixture of Conservative and Liberal ideals, holding Conservative views on some issues and Liberal views on others. Given their mixed ideology, predicting how a Moderate will fall on an issue is as difficult as predicting the weather.

Within the media, the terms Independent and Moderate are often used interchangeably. This is incorrect. Moderates are not necessarily Independents and Independents are not necessarily Moderates.[10]

---

[*]. If you are still uncertain as to which ideological label applies to you, take the Pew Research Center test at http://people-press.org/typology/quiz

Independent is a term used for party affiliation; Moderate is a termed used with ideology. Independents are not affiliated with either the Republican or Democrat political parties, but can be Conservative, Liberal, or Moderate; Moderates have an ideology that is a mixture of Conservative and Liberal, but can be either Republican, Democrat, or Independent. When examining the poll data, it is very important NOT to equate Moderates with Independents.

Ideological Make-up

Americans are split between the ideological camps as reported by Gallup on December 16, 2010:[11]

Conservatives: 40%

Moderates: 35%

Liberals: 21%

More Americans label themselves Conservative than any other ideology, with Moderate being a close second. Almost twice as many Americans label themselves Conservative as do Liberal. These numbers do not constitute a clear majority, but they do indicate that the electorate definitely leans toward conservative ideals.

Combine Party Affiliation with Ideology

Not all Conservatives are Republicans and not all Liberals are Democrats. It is tantalizing to make that assumption, after all, look at the poll numbers presented so far:

Party Affiliation		Ideology
Republican: 34.3%	---------	Conservatives: 40%
Democrat: 33.1%	----------	Liberal: 21%
Independent: 32.6%	-------	Moderate: 35%

Very close but too easy. Let's break down the numbers. Within each party, the ideology breaks down as:[11]

	Republican	Democrat	Independent
Conservative	72%	19%	36%
Liberal	4%	40%	19%
Moderate	23%	39%	41%

Table 2: Ideology by Party Affiliation

A couple of surprises pop out from this table: only 40% of Democrats label themselves Liberal; and almost twice as many Independents label themselves Conservative as Liberal. Now for some math. If we randomly take 1,000 voting Americans, we should get 343 Republicans, 331 Democrats, and 326 Independents per the breakdown by party affiliation. Applying the percentages listed in Table 2, we get the following numbers per 1,000 Americans:

	Republican	Democrat	Independent	Totals
Conservative	247	63	117	**427**
Liberal	14	132	62	**208**
Moderate	79	129	134	**342**
Totals	340	324	313	**977**

Table 3: Number of Americans by category for every 1,000 voters.

Of the 1,000 Americans, 427 label themselves Conservative, 208 label themselves Liberal, 342 label themselves Moderate, and the remaining 23 don't know. Translated to a percentage:

42.7% are Conservative

20.8% are Liberal

34.2% are Moderate

These numbers echo the ideology poll previously mentioned, as they should. This exercise confirms that the largest group of Americans call themselves Conservative by a 2:1 ratio over Liberals.

Still, Conservatives do not constitute a majority voting block according to the numbers. To create a majority vote requires a few Moderates to vote with the Conservatives or 85% of the Moderates to vote with the Liberals. If the Moderates split evenly between conservative and liberal candidates, the conservative candidate will have a majority voting block.

This conclusion is agreed to by Zogby:

> "There exists a real possibility that making the Republican party more conservative will expand its base by luring some of the independents into the fold."[10]

Summary

The previous analysis does not lend itself to declaring a majority in either party affiliation nor ideology. That more Americans call themselves Conservative is true. That the least number of Americans call themselves Liberal is also true. So it is how Independents and Moderates vote that will constitute the majority.

This is a very muddy picture. Let's see if the issues will help clear this up.

Chapter 3

Issues: Constitutional

"We, the people are the rightful masters of both Congress and
the courts, not to overthrow the Constitution, but to
overthrow men who pervert the Constitution."[1]

Abraham Lincoln

Our Founding Fathers revolted against the heavy-handed, impersonal monarchy that was the British government. With no political power, Americans took up arms and fought and died for individual liberty and unalienable rights. To prevent the excesses of big government, they created a small government with limited and carefully enumerated powers.

Today, do we see a small government with limited powers? The Federal Government had a 2010 budget of $3,456,000,000,000.[2] Too many zeros. Try this: $3.456 trillion dollars. Of which, $1.293 trillion is deficit (new debt) accumulated in just 1 year![2]

Our state governments spent $1.323 trillion dollars in 2009.[2] The local governments spent $1.59 trillion dollars in 2009.[2]

Assuming state and local government expenditures were similar in 2010, that is a total annual federal, state, and local government spending of $6.369 trillion dollars. The total economic output for the United States in 2010 (known as the GDP) was $14.66 trillion dollars.[2] Government spending for 2010 was 43% of total economic output. Small government? Limited powers?

How about the idea of $6.369 trillion dollars ripped from the purses and wallets of working Americans? Okay, deficits lower that number since the governments are spending $6.369 trillion dollars but not collecting all of it. Think about this: in 2010 our governments spent at a pace that requires taxing each American household $56,600 per year to cover the expenditures!* Frankly, I don't have that to give to the government. Do you?

---

*. According to the latest census data,[3] the U.S. population of 308,745,538 reside in
    112,611,029 households. That is $56,600 per household.

The Constitution created a government where the people are *supposed* to restrain the size, scope, and direction of the government. That occurs when the elected representatives listen to the people and do not saddle the government with powers beyond the scope of the Constitution. If they don't listen, the people are to vote them from office and elect representatives who will.

So, what are the people saying about the government?

Our Government

As previously mentioned, 83% of Americans do not believe the government represents them.[4] Let's dig a little deeper. Look at these horrifying numbers in 2011:

> Only 9% of us give Congress positive marks.[5]
>
> 75% say they do not share President Obama's political views.[6]
>
> 75% say the government is leading the country in the wrong direction.[7]

Americans believe their President doesn't represent their views, Congress is inept, and together they are leading us in a direction that will adversely affect the country. We also believe our leaders fail to put the country first:

> 82% of Americans believe the primary focus of their elected representative is to get re-elected.[8]

Not work for the people, not represent the people, not provide moral and intelligent leadership for the good of all, no, we believe our representatives just want to be re-elected and keep their positions of power and prestige. This is a far cry from the self-sacrificing concept of public service. Unfortunately, the people we elected over the years have earned our skepticism. You would think getting re-elected would require our representatives to work for us, with us, and in a manner that we approve of. Apparently not.

The Constitution

Some of our leaders have called the Constitution irrelevant and old-fashioned, no longer pertinent to modern society. A Supreme Court judge even suggested our laws should not be based on the Constitution but on the laws of foreign lands.[9] These people don't represent us:

90% of Americans say the Constitution is still relevant to modern life.[10]

Here is the Constitutional oath used to swear in a Supreme Court justice (and the President):

> "I, _____, do solemnly swear (or affirm) that I will support and defend the Constitution of the United States against all enemies, foreign and domestic; that I will bear true faith and allegiance to the same; that I take this obligation freely, without any mental reservation or purpose of evasion; and that I will well and faithfully discharge the duties of the office on which I am about to enter. So help me God."[12]

> *Constitutional Oath*

But:

> Only 38% of us believe the Supreme Court rules by the laws of the Constitution.[11]

A majority of Americans do not believe that the justices take the Constitutional Oath seriously. Unfortunately, Supreme Court justices are appointed for life. Our representatives? That's another matter. If 90% of us say the Constitution is relevant, perhaps our representatives and presidents should believe that too. Unfortunately:

> Only 39% believe the government is acting within the laws of the Constitution.[11]

Almost two-thirds of us believe that the government has exceeded its Constitutional mandate and is operating unconstitutionally! The Constitution has this introduction:

> "We the people of the United States, in Order to form a more perfect Union, establish Justice, insure domestic Tranquility, provide for the common defense, promote the general Welfare, and secure the Blessings of Liberty to ourselves and our Posterity, do ordain and establish this Constitution for the United States of America."

> *United States Constitution*

The words, "promote the general welfare" is one phrase the Federal government uses to greatly expand its powers. If the new powers are for the general welfare of the people, they are constitutional. The writers of the Constitution disagree with this argument:

> "Congress has not unlimited powers to provide for the general welfare, but only those specifically enumerated."[13]
>
> *Thomas Jefferson*

> "With respect to the two words 'general welfare,' I have always regarded them as qualified by the detail of powers connected with them. To take them in a literal and unlimited sense would be a metamorphosis of the Constitution..."[14]
>
> *James Madison*

Our Founding Fathers designed a small and limited government, which is now large and expansive. Today, Americans are thinking more like our Founders:

> 68% want smaller government and lower taxes.[15]

Americans want the Constitution to be relevant, we want the government to act within the limits of the Constitution, and we want a smaller government to exist within those limits.

Individual Rights

The Declaration of Independence states that each person has unalienable rights to life, liberty, and the pursuit of happiness. The Constitution and the Bill of Rights further define these principles, and are designed to protect the rights of the citizens. Yet today, here we are:

> 53% of Americans believe the government is a threat to individual rights.[16]

A majority of Americans believe the government is the enemy of our rights. The rights Americans died to create and protect. More laws like banning smoking in privately owned cars (Arkansas, California, Hawaii, Louisiana, Maine and Oregon), banning trans fats from restaurant food (New York City, Philadelphia, and others), and taking private property by eminent domain, may fuel American's fear of our government.

Despite an economy in a prolonged slump, the housing market in a shambles, inflation rising, and state and local governments broke, Americans say this:

59% say that protecting individual rights is more important than managing the economy or promoting social justice.[16]

Protecting individual rights is supremely important to Americans, yet 53% believe that the government created to protect us is a threat. Are the majority of us conspiracy theorists? Not likely.

Summary

All of this paints a very bleak picture of how the majority of Americans view the performance of our government:

- Congress is woefully inadequate

- President Obama does not share our political views

- The country is headed in the wrong direction, again.

- Our representatives are more interested in keeping their jobs then doing the right (and hard) things for our country

- The U.S. Constitution is relevant today, but our government is no longer bound by the Constitution

- Our government is a threat to individual rights

- Protecting individual rights is more important than the economy or social justice

Let's move on to fiscal (money) issues.

Chapter 4

Issues: Fiscal

"We must not let our rulers load us with perpetual debt...Taxation follows that, and in its train wretchedness and oppression."[1]

Thomas Jefferson

In Chapter 2, we discussed Conservative, Moderate, and Liberal in terms of general ideology. These labels also define our position on fiscal issues.

Fiscal Conservatives tend to want lower taxes, lower spending, smaller government, and no debt. They lean to the writings of Adam Smith in *The Wealth of Nations* (1776). While it is truly impossible to sum up the 1,000 page book in a couple of sentences, the terms capitalism and laissez-faire provide a good start:

> One of the guiding principles of capitalism, this doctrine (laissez-faire) claims that an economic system should be free from government intervention or moderation, and be driven only by the market forces.[2]

Smith believed that the market forces would eventually correct any imbalances in the economy and that free markets would provide the best prosperity for the greatest number of citizens. Market corrections, known as boom-and-bust cycles and sometimes leading to short recessions, was the balance being restored from an imbalanced and speculative position.

Fiscal Liberals want higher taxes, higher spending, larger government, and limited debt. They lean to the writings of John Maynard Keynes in *General Theory of Employment, Interest, and Money* (1936). He argued that in downturns the government should interfere in the markets and greatly increase spending to create temporary jobs.* Over time, his theory has been

---

*. For an in-depth analysis of how Hoover, FDR, and Keynesian economics deepened and lengthened the Depression, see Robert Higgs' article *Regime Uncertainty: Why the Great Depression Lasted So Long and Why Prosperity Resumed after the War* published in the Spring, 1997 edition of *The Independent Review.*

expanded to justify large government, high taxes, and government control at all times.

Fiscal Moderates are a mixture of these two economic theories. Americans break down with regard to fiscal issues as follows:[3]

Fiscal Conservatives: 44%

Fiscal Moderates: 40%

Fiscal Liberals: 11%

With only 11% of the population representing Fiscal Liberals, how did our representatives create the spending and debt numbers outlined in the beginning of Chapter 3?

Type of Economy

For generations, we have discussed the merits of capitalism vs. socialism vs. communism. Before we see how Americans fall on this issue, let's define the terms:

Capitalism: Economic system characterized by the following: private property ownership; individuals and companies are allowed to compete for their own economic gain; and free market forces determine the prices of goods and services. Such a system is based on the premise of separating the state and business activities. Capitalists believe that markets are efficient and should thus function without interference, and the role of the state is to regulate and protect.[4]

Socialism: Economic system which is based on cooperation rather than competition and which utilizes centralized planning and distribution.[5] A theory or system of social organization that advocates ownership and control of production and distribution of capital, land, etc. in the community as a whole; the stage following capitalism in the transition of a society to communism.[6]

Communism: A system of social organization in which all economic and social activity is controlled by a totalitarian state dominated by a single and self-perpetuating political party.[7]

There is no need to spend a lot of time on communism. Here's why:

87% say capitalism works better than communism.[8]

80% say capitalism is better for the middle-class.[8]

73% say communism has failed.[8]

83% say capitalism is *morally superior* to communism.[8]

Communism is not on the voter's mind, but the debate between capitalism and socialism is running strong. A thorough examination between the two would fill a book (and has) but a brief overview is included here to clarify the positions:[9]

Topic	Capitalism	Socialism
Society	In capitalism, society is ruled by individuals; socialism is ruled by the state.	In socialism, society is ruled by the people; capitalism is ruled by money.
Property	The right to own property (land, business, and goods) is central to man's existence. Private ownership gives individuals security and a means to control their own affairs.	Property belongs to all men and should be owned by the community, not individuals. Capitalism leads to gross inequality.
Markets	Free markets: the market determines pricing of goods and labour. Individuality is valued and rewards are based on ability, work ethic, and risk-taking.	Controlled markets: Central planning spreads the wealth to prevent the rich from getting richer and the poor poorer.
Regulations	Most capitalists accept a role for state regulation to prevent market rigging and to help those in absolute poverty.	Central planning assumes control by the state.

Topic	Capitalism	Socialism
Government control	Governments move too slow and therefore innovation is missed, resulting in a lower standard of living for all. When the government controls the economy, any mistake causes all to suffer.	Socialist economies are planned, thereby eliminating the boom and bust cycles of capitalism. Socialism guides with the aim of human happiness not individual success. To accomplish this requires an element of social control.
Monopolies	Monopolies stifle competition and regulation should prevent them from occurring. Competition results in better products at lower costs.	The state is a monopoly but benign.
Individual Rights	Protects and encourages individual rights.	Seeks the good of the people even if that means overriding individual rights.
Work/Reward	When work is uncoupled from reward, or an artificial safety net provides a high standard of living to the unproductive, society suffers.	The impulse to share wealth and material among the community is one of the purest mankind can experience.
Redistribution of Wealth	Steals from those who are productive and gives to those who are unproductive.	Necessary for fairness.

Table 4: Comparison of capitalism and socialism

The American economy is no longer a strict capitalistic economy. Our government provides Social Security payments, Medicare/Medicaid coverage, welfare, and many other programs that require the redistribution of wealth. These programs fall under the socialism heading, not capitalism. We have a "mixed" economy.

Our economy may be more mixed than we realize. Look at this partial listing of the 10 steps for a peaceful transition to communism as listed by Karl

Marx and Friedrich Engels in *The Communist Manifesto*.[10] Information in the parentheses is added by the author:

1. Abolition of property in land and application of all rents of land to public purposes. *(The Federal Government currently owns almost 30% of all U.S. land*[11] *and government-related entities backed 96.5% of all home loans during the first quarter of 2010.*[12]*)*

2. A heavy progressive or graduated income tax. *(Established in 1913.)*

3. Abolition of all right of inheritance. *(Estate tax established in 1916.)*

5. Centralization of credit in the hands of the state by means of a national bank with state capital and an exclusive monopoly. *(Federal Reserve Bank established in 1913.***)*

10. Free education for all children in public schools.

Most Americans, myself included, do not consider our state-sponsored education system a step toward socialism and communism, yet Marx and Engels did. Our economy is indeed "mixed." The question before us today is: do we abandon capitalism and free-fall into socialism or do we put the brakes on socialism and live with a mixed economy? Here's what we say:

60%-18% say capitalism is better than socialism.[13]

58% have a negative view of socialism.[14]

86% have a positive view of free enterprise.[14]

84% have a positive view of entrepreneurs.[14]

Clearly, a majority of Americans prefer capitalism, the entrepreneurial spirit, the rights to property, the individualism of free markets, and reward for work performed. Thomas Jefferson would be pleased with us:

"I predict future happiness for Americans if they can prevent the government from wasting the labors of the people under the pretense of taking care of them."[15]

Thomas Jefferson

---

*. President Woodrow Wilson had good years in 1913 and 1916 pushing his progressive agenda.

It is interesting to note that big business does not fare so well:

> 49%-49% split on positive vs. negative views for big business.[14]

Apparently when an entrepreneur uses free enterprise to grow a big business, they lose our support. Either big business earned this reputation or the media successfully demonized them.

We clearly prefer a mixed economy with some regulation to prevent abuses and with a safety net to help those truly in need. Each year the government debates which side of our mixed economy gets the most attention. The budget battles in Congress during 2011 were not only about deficits and debt ceilings, but also about how Americans view the scope and purpose of government.

Deficit and Spending Cuts

> 95% of Americans say it is important to reduce the deficit.[16]

That's pretty clear, but we are not confident that our representatives think the same way:

> 70% of us believe that voters are more willing to make the hard choices needed to reduce spending than elected politicians are.[17]

Americans want deficit reduction, but doubt our representatives will make it happen. Given the deal just completed on the debt ceiling, we are right.

The next question is, how do Americans want the deficit to be reduced? Are we willing to let the government take more of our money in taxes? Do we want a government that provides less services? Which services are important to us and which are not? What do we believe caused the deficits in the first place? The last question is the easiest to answer:

> 83% of us blame the deficit on too much spending, not that taxes are too low.[17]

> Only 22% say that low taxes caused the deficit.[18]

These numbers are from two different polls so they don't add up. However, out-of-control spending gets the nod as the culprit to deficits. No surprise there. We know our taxes are high and deficits are still soaring.

Americans are also realistic about fixing the deficit:

85% say it is necessary to reduce the deficit with both spending
cuts and tax increases.[18]

Unfortunately, while we have a good grasp on the big picture, we have no clear idea of where to make spending cuts. This table reflects our view on cutting the deficit and is reproduced from a 2011 Gallup poll:[19]

Area to Cut	Favor	Oppose	No Opinion
Foreign Aid	59	37	4
Arts and Sciences	46	52	2
Aid to farmers	44	53	3
Homeland Security	42	56	3
National Defense	42	57	1
Anti-poverty programs	39	55	6
Medicare	38	61	1
Social Security	34	64	2
Education	32	67	2

Table 5: Favor/Oppose where to cut the budget

This poll suggests that we will only support spending cuts for foreign aid. Unfortunately, foreign aid is only a small portion of total spending. We have a problem: spending must be reduced, but no budget item with significant spending has majority support to cut. Americans may have a viable solution though it gets no press or consideration: what if government productivity increased without cutting services?

In 1984, the Grace Commission presented a report to President Reagan which concluded:

"One-third of all taxes is consumed by waste and inefficiency in
the Federal Government."[20]

One-third! In the 2010 Federal budget, that translates into $1.152 trillion dollars! Nearly equivalent to the entire budget deficit for that year! The inefficiency of government is staggering. No polls have been conducted asking the American people if they would first prefer a reduction in government waste and inefficiency before cutting services and raising taxes, but how would you vote?

By the way, Congress ignored the Grace Commission report.

Taxes

The American people are not tax-a-phobic. We understand the need for taxes and we want the necessary government services our taxes provide, like a strong military. However, we do not believe taxes are good for the economy:

> 53% believe raising taxes hurts the economy.[21]

The majority of Americans believe high taxes are bad and yet every year our government heatedly discusses raising taxes. And the majority believes our taxes are already too high:

> 68% want lower taxes and smaller government.[22]

Redistribution of Wealth

A large part of the discussion on taxes is the redistribution of wealth; money taken from the rich and middle class and given to the poor to even out the financial landscape. Redistribution is a socialist concept, but capitalists also agree a safety net is needed for the truly destitute. Americans have to decide if redistribution of wealth means helping the poor, or whether it's a way for the government to control the wealth of America through the guise of doing social good.

This issue has been in American politics since the beginning of our country. Our Founding Fathers said:

> "I cannot undertake to lay my finger on that article of the Constitution which granted a right to Congress of expending, on objects of benevolence, the money of their constituents."[23]

James Madison

> "That is not a just government ... where the property which a man has in his personal safety and personal liberty, is violated by arbitrary seizures of one class of citizens for the service of the rest."[24]

James Madison

"To take from one, because it is thought his own industry and
   that of his fathers has acquired too much...is to violate...the
   free exercise of their industry and the fruits acquired by it."[25]

Thomas Jefferson

"I am doing good for the poor, but I differ in opinion of the
   means. I think the best way of doing good to the poor, is not
   making them easy in poverty, but leading or driving them out
   of it."[26]

Benjamin Franklin

Madison and Jefferson are defending the right to property and extolling individual industry, while Franklin is saying it is better to teach a man to fish than to give him a fish. Given that our Founders believed in individualism, their thoughts on redistribution of wealth are not surprising. Today, Americans are mixed on the redistribution of wealth:

49%-47% do not want wealth redistributed through taxes and
   government programs.[27]

A breakdown of this outcome reveals an expected result:[27]

Category	Do Not Redistribute	Redistribute
Republicans	69%	28%
Independents	53%	43%
Democrats	26%	71%
Income less 30K/year	32%	63%
Income 30-75K/year	47%	51%
Income over 75K/year	67%	31%

Table 6: Redistribution of Wealth

Those with less want those with more to pay higher taxes and those with more want to keep their earnings. Since more Republicans are Conservative and more Democrats are Liberal, this breakdown is no surprise. The Moderates opinion was not reflected in this poll.

So America is truly divided on the issue of redistribution of wealth. Since Americans also want lower taxes and a smaller government, exactly how to accomplish this without affecting the redistribution of wealth is unclear. Undoubtably, this issue will continue to be controversial in the foreseeable future, but we know where our President stands:

> "...when you spread the wealth around, it's good for
> everybody..."[28]

Barack Obama

Bailouts

In response to the economic downturn beginning in 2008, the Federal government financed numerous banks, investment houses, and businesses including Goldman Sachs and General Motors. The government now owns a portion of these businesses. Constitutionality aside, our government embarked on this policy despite what we thought:

> 71% view the bank bailouts unfavorably.[29]

> 59%-25% view the bailouts to the banks, insurance companies,
> and the auto industry as bad policy.[30]

Most Americans are not economists and we are not privy to inside information on the stability of the economy and our monetary system. We rely on the experts to guide us and make policy decisions aimed at economic health. But Americans realized that when Ben Bernanke, Chairman of the Federal Reserve, and other economic leaders said they had no idea the crisis of 2008 was coming, and that there was *no way* to predict the coming crisis, we were not being told the truth.

A competent economist couldn't predict an economic crises of such magnitude? Really? Also, Economic Commentator Peter Schiff warned us in his book *Crashproof* that the crisis was on its way two years before the credit crunch. Today, Americans have little confidence in our economic leaders:

> Only 29% of us have confidence in Ben Bernanke.[31]

> Only 38% of us have confidence in the President's economic
> advisors.[31]

> 74% of us want an audit of the Federal Reserve.[31]

Back to the bailouts. By more than a 2:1 margin, Americans did not want the government to bailout the banks, insurance companies, and auto companies.[30] It gets worse. We believe that those who caused the crisis are being rewarded:

> 68% of us believe that the bailout money went to those who
> caused the problems.[32]

Americans believe our taxpayer money was improperly used to bailout those either so greedy or so incompetent that they created a financial meltdown. And we disapprove.

Summary

The purpose of this book is to determine who the majority is in America and where we stand on major issues. On the issues covered in this chapter:

- Fiscal Conservatives out-number Fiscal Liberals 3-to-1

- Capitalism is the preferred type of economic system

- A majority want lower taxes and smaller government

- Deficit reduction is paramount

- The deficit is due to out-of-control Congressional spending

- No clear consensus exists on where to cut the budget

- Higher taxes is bad for the economy

- Private ownership of business by the government, and government interference in saving a business from bankruptcy, is bad for the country

- The jury is still out on the redistribution of wealth

In this chapter, we briefly covered our views on fiscal issues. Next we will discuss foreign affairs, health care, energy policy, immigration, terrorism, and a view on state governments and unions.

Chapter 5

Issues: Healthcare, Energy, and More

"The way to have a safe government is not to trust it all to the
one, but to divide it among the many, distributing to everyone
exactly the functions in which he is competent..."[1]

Thomas Jefferson

Today, the headlines are dominated by the economy and the upcoming Presidential election, but that is only the latest media frenzy. The world is still turning and Americans have views on all of it. Let's start with an easy one.

Healthcare

In 2010, Congress passed a universal, must-have-by-law healthcare bill. Prior to the vote, Americans said:

50%-47% that healthcare is not the government's responsibility.[2]

One month after the bill became law, Zogby reported on April 21, 2010:

51%-44% of voters oppose the Healthcare Reform Act.[3]

And into 2011:

53% of us say to repeal the Healthcare Reform Act.[4]

49%-32% say the Healthcare Reform Act is bad for the country.[4]

Rasmussen states: "The majority of voters have favored repeal
every week but one since Congress passed the health care law
in late March 2010."[4]

Despite the November 2010 elections, the Senate and President Obama will not consider repealing the healthcare law in favor of new regulations covering uninsured Americans. Insured Americans are not the issue:

79%-2% rate their existing heath insurance coverage as good or
excellent.[4]

The problem of uninsured Americans is shared by all facets of our population, Conservative, Liberal, Moderate, Democrat, Republican, Independent. We differ not about access to health care, but in how to achieve it. Despite majority opposition, the Healthcare Reform Act was passed. Another new program established without the consent of the governed.

Energy Policy

Energy policy is the one area where our views drastically changed over the last few years. Many factors have impacted this:

- The realization that environmental concerns will significantly raise the price of gasoline, natural gas, and electricity

- The debunking of man-made global warming theory by the global warming scientists who admitted they cooked the numbers to get the results they wanted

- The huge snafu of using corn for fuel (ethanol), thereby raising corn prices and reducing the amount available for food

The polls do not tell us which ranks as the leading factor, however, a significant shift has occurred:

In 2001, 52%-36% of us agreed to protect the environment even if that meant limiting energy production.[5]

In 2011, 50%-41% of us agree to increase energy production even if the environment suffers.[5]

Conservation is not in vogue either:

58%-32% approve finding more energy rather than reducing consumption.[6]

Americans work hard to establish and maintain their standard of living. Conservation through efficiency gains is great; conservation by lowering our standard of living is a slap in the face. It is difficult to take conservationists seriously since none of them give away their energy consuming items and live in a cave. Instead, Al Gore lectures us while living in his 10,000 square foot home that consumes more energy in one month than the average house does in a year.[7]

As the price of a gallon of gas consistently exceeds $3.00 a gallon for regular, and the EPA is implementing regulations that may significantly increase the cost of electricity from coal-fired plants, Americans are coming to grips with cost versus environmental good. In fact:

> 72% of us are not willing to pay more than $10/month in extra energy costs to reduce emissions.[8]

Even before the scientists admitted to lying about global warming, Americans were not interested in paying for it. In 2009:

> 56% did not want to pay more energy costs to fight global warming.[9]

Between the scientists cooking the data and the simple fact that none of the catastrophic results have occurred as predicted, Americans no longer buy into man-made global warming:

> 51%-19% blame extreme weather on natural trends, not human activity.[10]

> 63%-26% say we are in a normal weather cycle, not global warming.[11]

Energy policy is not just an issue of conservation or global warming, it is also a security issue. Our dependence on foreign oil has put the U.S. at the mercy of unstable, unfriendly Middle Eastern governments. We don't need to be experts on foreign policy or Homeland security to see the potential danger in relying on foreign sources of oil:

> Over 60% of us want to decrease dependence on imported energy.[12]

Recently, our government halted all off-shore oil drilling in response to an accident on a drilling platform. Most of the spilled oil was consumed by the ocean before it reached shore, but along some shorelines it was pretty messy and wildlife suffered. However, only months after the accident:

> 67% of us approve of off-shore drilling.[13]

Meanwhile, workers are unemployed, Seahawk Drilling has declared bankruptcy, and the price of gasoline has spiked. And that's just off-shore drilling; we have substantial oil under the mainland that our government prevents us from drilling. This is not to say Americans overwhelmingly approve of energy that produces carbon emissions:

66% of us emphasize the development of alternative energy sources.[5]

62% favor nuclear power and the building of more nuclear plants.[14]

In summary, the majority of Americans want energy independence, greater domestic energy production, and continued research into cleaner energy sources. Despite the majority stance on these issues, we elected a President who said during the 2008 campaign:

> "If somebody wants to build a coal-fired plant they can, its just that it will bankrupt them because they [are] going to be charged a huge sum for all that green-house gas that's being emitted."[15]

Barack Obama

Immigration

To discuss immigration, let's define the terms:

- Immigration is the lawful process of a citizen from another country coming into the U.S. to live and work. This process is governed by our laws and the appropriate government agencies.

- Illegal immigration is an unlawful practice where citizens from another country come into the U.S. without engaging in the due process for immigration. Many can buy false identification and other papers.

- Illegal aliens are citizens of another country who entered the U.S. illegally.

In the media, those who oppose illegal immigration are portrayed as opposing any immigration. This is not true:

57% of Americans believe legal immigration is a good thing.[16]

The issue of illegal immigration has been a heated debate for years. In 2008:

83% of Americans were angry at the Federal Government concerning illegal immigration.[17]

In all the debate over the years, here is what Americans think:

64% of us rate illegal immigration as an extremely serious issue.[18]

89% believe it is important to close the Mexican border.[19]

90% believe it is important to develop a plan for existing illegal aliens.[19]

62% believe illegal immigration costs us (the taxpayer) too much money.[18]

It's pretty clear that we want illegal immigration to stop and a plan put into place to deal with existing illegal aliens. There are a couple of legal loopholes we want closed too:

79% say illegal aliens do not have the same rights as American citizens.[20]

65% believe that the babies of illegal aliens born in the U.S. should not automatically be U.S. citizens.[21]

Americans cherish our citizenship. Our citizenship grants us the ideals of the Declaration of Independence and the laws of the Constitution and the Bill of Rights. Immigrants have come to America for 200 years for our citizenship.

My grandparents came to America as young children from Italy. Their parents did not speak English and my grandmother started public school without understanding our language.[*] Her daughter, my mother, grew up in an English speaking household (except for the loud discussions between her parents), and I don't know a word of Italian. My family assimilated into America and while we hang on to some family recipes, my grandparents let go of their roots to be American citizens. This is the preferred evolution of immigrant families in America:

73% of us believe immigrants should adopt U.S. culture.[22]

English has become a battlefield over assimilation. Rasmussen states:

"American's overwhelmingly believe that English should be the official language of the United States."[22]

But we elected a President who said during the 2008 campaign:

---

[*]. The teacher did not speak Italian, nor was expected to.

"Instead of worrying about whether immigrants can learn
   English, Americans need to make sure your child can speak
   Spanish."[23]

Barack Obama

Also:

58% of us want English-only ballots for voting.[22]

74% want voter ID to make sure only citizens are voting.[22]

In accordance with this and other security issues, the states are passing new, tough immigration laws. Arizona began the trend and the Federal government promptly sued them to prevent the law from being enacted. Americans were not pleased:

50%-33% oppose the Federal government lawsuit against the
   Arizona immigration law.[24]

Our government and Americans are at odds concerning illegal immigration.

Terrorists

As odd as it sounds, we debate whether foreign terrorists should be given the rights of U.S. citizens. While the government has vacillated on the issue, we have not:

73%-17% say do not give terrorists the rights of U.S. citizens.[25]

We view terrorism as a military issue:

60% of us say terrorists should be tried before military tribunals
   not in U.S. courts.[25]

Our government recently planned to prosecute a terrorist in a New York City court, but the backlash, security concerns, and the willing martyrdom of Islamic terrorists nixed the plan. Score one for the majority opinion.

While some are vastly disappointed that the Guantanamo Prison is still open, the majority of us approve:

58% say do not close the prison at Guantanamo Bay.[25]

Americans believe that terrorists are military combatants, are not citizens, should not be tried in U.S. courts, and should stay in prison until tried by a military tribunal.

Americans understand that terrorism is a religious war and not caused by economic disparity, heavy-handed American foreign policy, or other ideas presented by the media. 225 years ago, Muslim terrorists acted as pirates and conducted raids against American ships. On March 28, 1786, Thomas Jefferson and John Adams wrote this after meeting with the terrorists:

> "The Ambassador answered us that it was founded on the Laws of their Prophet, that it was written in their Koran, that all nations who should not have acknowledged their authority were sinners, that it was their right and duty to make war upon them wherever they could be found..."[26]

This is the war of terrorism.

Foreign Affairs

One area that must fall under the umbrella of the Federal government is national defense and foreign affairs. The need for this speaks for itself: we couldn't possibly have the Governors of the 50 states independently deal with the leaders of other nations.

United Nations (UN)

We may live in a global economy and accept the economic realities that imposes on us, but Americans are very skeptical about the pseudo-global government that is the UN:

> 52% view the UN unfavorably.[27]

> Only 27% of us see the UN as an ally.[27]

Separate polls are not available on what Americans think about the UN call for a single world currency or the inability of the UN to enforce the sanctions that it passes. We do know we are not confident in UN military operations:

> 46%-18% say that UN involvement in Egypt will make the situation worse.[27]

Should we abandon ship? No:

63% of us say the U.S. should continue to participate in the UN.[27]

Why we should continue to participate was not discussed, but it is clear that we are uneasy with the UN and uncertain that the UN will promote American interests.

Israel

Since the inception of modern Israel, the U.S. has been a staunch ally. While we attempted to broker peace with the Palestinians and their various representatives, the security of Israel was always paramount. Recently, our President has vacillated on the security of Israel, even suggesting that Israel go back to the borders prior to the 1967 war, a situation that experts say would be very dangerous for Israel. However, the American people are not vacillating. Over the last 11 years, we strongly favor Israel over Palestine[27] with the 2011 polls coming in as:

> 68% favorable toward Israel, 19% favorable toward the Palestine Authority.[28]

However, we are not convinced that the Israel/Palestine problem is our problem:

> Only 23% of us believe it is our job to find a solution to the Israel/Palestine conflict.[12]

Just as we do not turn to Israel for help with illegal immigration and the Mexican border, we are not certain we should be involved in Israel's border problems.

Libya

As of this writing, the U.S. is involved in UN military action in Libya supporting the fighters against the recently deposed Gaddafi. One of the first steps of the new government was to declare Sharia law. Such governments are, to date, generally not friendly to the U.S. Prior to entering into the conflict:

> 63% of us said to stay out and not join the UN in the intervention.[29]

We had our doubts about the outcome:

70% of us were concerned that a new Libyan government will be hostile to the U.S.[30]

In fact, Americans are very skeptical over the role of promoting democracy (republics) abroad and defending human rights abroad:

Only 13% of us believe we should promote democracy abroad.[12]

Only 24% of us believe we should promote human rights abroad.[12]

Yet the lives of our soldiers and our money are being sent oversees against the wish of the majority.

Affairs of the States

It was a great shock to me, being born with a large Federal government firmly established, to learn that the intention of our Founding Fathers was strong state governments and a weak federal government. It was not until I read the Constitution as a middle-aged adult that I saw how disordered our government systems are compared to the intent of our Founding Fathers:

"…[The] government of the United States is a definite government, confined to specified objects. It is not like the state governments, whose powers are more general."[31]

James Madison

"When all government, domestic and foreign, in little as in great things, shall be drawn to Washington as the center of all power, it will render powerless the checks provided of one government on another and will become as venal and oppressive as the government from which we separated."[32]

Thomas Jefferson

The usurpation of power by the Federal government from the States would make interesting reading but is beyond the scope of this book. However, the States are fighting back and have the support of the people:

50%-33% oppose the Federal government lawsuit against the Arizona immigration law.[24]

A plurality of poll responders support state lawsuits against the Federal health care plan.[33]

We also support the states as they assert themselves against the public unions:

> 52% agree that state legislatures can void collective bargaining agreements to balance state budgets.[34]

> 67% agree that states can cut salaries to balance state budgets.[34]

> 62% agree the states can reduce the number of state employees to balance state budgets.[35]

The States are fighting back.

Government Responsibilities

The Constitution enumerates the limited responsibilities of the Federal government. Over the years, our perception of the government's responsibilities has changed. Putting aside the restraints of the Constitution, what do Americans perceive as the responsibilities of our Federal government?

In June, 2011, Pew Research asked Americans which responsibilities were important for the government to perform. Here's the results:[12]

Responsibility	% of Americans indicating important
Protect U.S. jobs	84%
Protect us from terrorism	81%
Reduce our dependence on imported energy	67%
Improve foreign relations	46%
Reduce military commitments	46%
Destroy terrorist groups overseas	44%
Deal with global warming	29%
Promote human rights abroad	24%
Solve the Israeli/Palestine conflict	23%

Responsibility	% of Americans indicating important
Promote democracy abroad	13%

Table 7: What Americans want the Federal government to do

Only employment, national security, and domestic energy production have majority support. The rest are not so important to Americans.

Summary

The purpose of this book is to determine who is the majority in America and where do they stand on the issues. On the issues covered in this chapter, the majority of Americans say:

- Health care is not the government's responsibility

- Repeal the Healthcare Reform Act

- Increase domestic energy production even at the expense of the environment

- It is not okay to increase energy costs to reduce emissions

- Illegal aliens do not have the same rights as American citizens

- The Mexican border should be closed

- Tough immigration laws are necessary and should be enforced

- Immigrants should assimilate into American culture

- Foreign terrorists are not citizens, should not be given the rights of citizens, and should be tried before military tribunals

- The UN is not our ally

- Israel is our ally

- We should not be involved in Libya

- The states need to exercise their power

This chapter covered our views on many different issues. Additional issues are still to be dealt with, however, to adequately discuss these we need to see where America stands on religion.

Chapter 6

Issues: Religious

No power over the freedom of religion...is delegated to the
United States by the Constitution.[1]

Thomas Jefferson

92% of Americans believe in God.[2]

Gallup Poll, June, 2011

When discussing politics, religion is a dirty word. Separation of church
and state precludes discussing or making policy based on religious principles
or beliefs. Our leaders rarely talk about God; our laws rarely include God in
the language. Talking about one's faith can be considered political suicide
and is certainly scorned in the media. 92% of us have allowed God to be
deleted from the discussion.

I take the bold step of mixing religion and politics because we *are* a
religious people and how we view many issues depends upon our faith.
Unfortunately, the media works very hard to suggest positions based on faith
is the realm of the weak-minded who are out-of-touch with modern life.
Religion is under attack, right down to revisionist history on the faith of our
Founding Fathers. More on that in a moment. First, here is what the law of
our land says on religion:

"Congress shall make no law respecting an establishment of
religion, or prohibiting the free exercises thereof,..."

United States Constitution, First Amendment

"...but no religious Test shall ever be required as a Qualification
to any Office or public Trust in the United States."

United States Constitution, Article VI

That is the sum total of what our Constitution says about religion. The
Federal government cannot create a government-sponsored religion nor
impede citizens from exercising their religion. Anyone of any faith can serve
as a public servant. From this, our courts have handed down decisions

concerning the 'separation of church and state,' right down to removing the Ten Commandments from public buildings and prohibiting manger scenes during Christmas.

Our Founding Fathers are attacked on two fronts concerning this issue:

- How could people who allowed slavery have a true faith

- They were not very religious people

This is not the forum for a discussion on slavery and faith. Slavery is an abomination and was outlawed in 1865 by Amendment 13 of the Constitution. The best we can say is that *some* of our Founding Fathers believed too well in an antiquated system. However, to dismiss their views on all topics is ridiculous and a practice that we do not adhere to in our own lives. We disagree with people all the time but respect their thoughts on other topics. Were our Founders wrong on slavery? Yes. Were they right on unalienable rights? You bet. Did they see the contradiction? Some did.

The second charge, that our Founding Fathers were not really religious people, is easily refuted. Even a cursory view of their writings shows just the opposite:

> "The moment the idea is admitted into society that property is not as sacred as the laws of God, and that there is not a force of law and public justice to protect it, anarchy and tyranny commence."[3]
>
> *John Adams*

> "The foundation of our national policy will be laid in the pure and immutable principles of private morality;...the propitious smiles of Heaven can never be expected on a nation that disregards the eternal rules of order and right which Heaven itself has ordained..."[4]
>
> *George Washington, First Inaugural Address*

> "And can the liberties of a nation be thought secure when we have removed their only firm basis, a conviction in the minds of the people that these liberties are the gift of God?"[1]
>
> *Thomas Jefferson*

Our Founder's believed they were acting in faith in the creation of the United States. That the laws protecting individual rights were ordained by

God. They believed that only a God-fearing, moral people could make this Great Experiment of a republic work:

> "Our Constitution was made only for a moral and religious people. It is wholly inadequate to the government of any other."[5]
>
> *John Adams*

Our Founding Fathers believed that divorcing faith from the government would doom our country. From that perspective, religion in America is crucial to our politics.

Our Faith

92% of Americans believe in God.[2]

7% of Americans are atheist.[2]

Our faith breaks down as follows according to Pew Forum:[6]

Faith	% of American Believers
Christian	78.4%
Jewish	1.7%
Muslim	0.6%
Buddhist	0.7%
Hindu	0.4%
Unaffiliated Believers	16.1%
Other	1.2%

Table 8: Americans by faith

Combine these percentages with the previous statistics, and for every 1,000 Americans, we break out as follows:

Faith	Number of Followers per 1,000 Americans
Christian	721
Jewish	16
Muslim	6
Buddhist	6
Hindu	4
Unaffiliated Believers	148
Other	11
Atheist	70

Table 9: Number of Americans per thousand by faith

America is not wholly a Christian nation, but the large majority is. And:

80% of the faithful say faith is important to their daily lives.[7]

70% say they want more religion in this country.[8]

59% site the declining influence of religion as bad for the country.[8]

The majority of Americans realize that disconnecting government from religious morals is bad policy. True, a government that presides over a nation of such diverse religious thought, even under the general label of Christianity, is a difficult proposition. But there is a huge difference between grappling with religious thought and acting as if it doesn't exist.

Our view of the political parties on this issue is not positive:

74% say that Democrats are not religion friendly.[8]

53% say that Republicans are not religion friendly.[8]

In a representative country where 80% say their faith is important to their daily lives, this represents a huge disconnect between the people and their government.

Issues

If faith is important to our daily lives, the natural conclusion is that faith will influence our position on the issues. This includes opinions on abortion, the death penalty, religion in schools, faith-based government programs, and same-sex marriage.

Abortion

A plurality of Americans support abortion as legal in all/most cases:

47%-45% say abortion should be legal.[9]

Recently, support for abortion has slipped. 2008 and 2009 saw the numbers move from 54%-41% to the above numbers. Whether this shift was influenced by the presidential campaign of 2008 was not discussed in the poll.

The importance of abortion as a campaign issue significantly fell between 2008 and 2009 across all political party affiliations and idealogies.[9] Only 26% of conservatives rate abortion as a critical issue.[9]

Death Penalty

Controversy continues to reign over the death penalty. The application of DNA testing to old cases, resulting in a handful of pardons, has stirred the waters and renewed the debate. Americans want to get it right and no one wants innocent people to be killed. The Constitution says this about the death penalty:

> No person shall be...deprived of life, liberty, or property, without due process of law;...
>
> *Bill of Rights, Amendment 5, passed 12/15/1791*

Amendment 5 clearly states that the government may deprive life with due process of law. Amendment 8 was passed on the same day:

> Excessive bail shall not be required, nor excessive fines imposed, nor cruel and unusual punishments inflicted.
>
> *Bill of Rights, Amendment 8, passed 12/15/1791*

Presumably Congress and the States did not see a conflict between these two amendments, as they passed on the same day. Americans don't either:

62%-32% of Americans support the death penalty for a murder conviction.[10]

This majority has fluctuated over the last 46 years, but the split was never less than 8 percentage points.[10] Despite the vast majority, death-row inmates languish for years, sometimes decades, as the appeal process delays execution and costs us millions of dollars. In contrast, the families of the victims are not supported by the government.

Religion in Schools

As a part of the separation of church and state, religion, including attempts to delete "under God" in the Pledge of Allegiance, has been removed from the public schools. The majority view of Americans is:

65% favor prayer in schools.[11]

69% say Liberals go too far to keep religion out of schools.[12]

74% say religious symbols should be allowed on government property.[13]

83% say Christmas displays should be allowed on government property.[14]

In the public schools, evolution has supplanted creationism as the origin of mankind. Americans are not happy:

58% want both evolutionary theory and biblical creationism to be taught in the public schools.[12]

The majority believes in creationism. First:

48%-42% believe that man evolved over time rather than was created as just man (biblical creationism).[15]

Second:

38% of evolutionists believe God guided the process to create man.[15]

The result is that 60% of Americans believe God guided the creation of mankind in one form or another. Only a minority of us believe strictly in evolution:

26% of us believe man evolved strictly through the process of natural selection.[15]

Schools are an environment of authority. What is taught affects how our children think (that is why Marx and Engels wanted public education, as quoted in chapter 4). We want our children to be exposed to options, and we don't want religion to be excluded.

Faith-based Government Programs

Faith-based government programs, implemented by President George Bush, are programs where the government gives money to charitable organizations to supply social services. This issue confuses the usually staunch positions of Liberals and Conservatives.

At first glance, these programs are in direct opposition to the separation of church and state, a strict line that Liberals usually adhere to. While these programs fulfill the liberal ideal of the government giving to the poor, it is not a direct line of giving since it involves a charitable organization. Yet, 83% of Democrats favor these programs.[16]

On the other side, Conservatives usually dislike government money used for charity, believing that the private sector can better serve the needs of the poor. Yet, 66% of Republicans support these programs.[16] Overall:

69% of Americans agree that the churches should get government funds to provide social services.[16]

Finally, a program that satisfies the ideology of Americans across the board.

Same-sex Marriage

The debate over same-sex marriage is still going strong in America. However, it is not popular:

54% oppose same-sex marriage.[17]

Over time, the opposition to same-sex marriage is diminishing. If the trends hold, the issue may eventually turn majority to the other side.

Summary

The purpose of this book is to determine who is the majority in America and where do they stand on the issues. On the issues covered in this chapter, the majority of Americans believe:

- God exists

- Jesus Christ is the Savior

- Faith is important to our daily lives

- We need more religion in this country

- The declining influence of religion is bad for the country

- Abortion should be legal

- The death penalty is proper for a murder conviction

- Prayer should be allowed in the schools

- Religious symbols should be allowed on government property

- Biblical creationism and evolutionary theory should both be taught in the public schools

- The churches should get government funds to provide social services

- Marriage is between a man and a woman

This concludes our study of the issues. Now it is time to answer the question: Who is the majority in America?

Chapter 7

We Are The Majority

"The fabric of (the) American empire ought to rest on the solid
basis of THE CONSENT OF THE PEOPLE. The streams
of national power ought to flow from that pure, original
fountain of all legitimate authority."[1]

Alexander Hamilton

We've covered party affiliation, ideology, and many issues to help identify who the majority in America is and what they believe. We have statistics and facts, so let's take a look at the cohesive whole.

Party Affiliation and Ideology

In both party affiliation and ideology, America is a pie just about cut into thirds:

Party Affiliation	%	Ideology	%
Republican	35.6	Conservative	40
Independent	30.4	Moderate	35
Democrat	34.0	Liberal	21

From these numbers, Americans lean toward the conservative and out number liberals almost 2:1.

Issues and Ideology

The following table lists the issues covered in these pages and rates the majority view as conservative or liberal per the outline in Chapter 2. It is difficult to be moderate on a single issue, one falls either into the conservative or the liberal side. Where do Americans fall? Let's see:

Majority Position	Conservative	Liberal
The U.S. Constitution is relevant today	X	
Lower taxes and smaller government	X	
Protecting individual rights is more important than social justice	X	
Government is a threat to individual rights	X	
Capitalism is the best type of economic system	X	
Deficit reduction is paramount	X	
Deficit is due to out-of-control government spending	X	
Government ownership of private business is bad for the country	X	
Redistribute wealth--split	X	X
Fiscal Conservatives out-number Fiscal Liberals 3-to-1	X	
No clear consensus exists on where to cut the budget	?	?
Higher taxes is bad for the economy	X	
Health care is not a government responsibility	X	
Repeal the Healthcare Reform Act	X	
Increase domestic energy production regardless of the effect on the environment	X	
Do not reduce emissions by raising energy costs	X	
Illegal aliens do not have the rights of American citizens	X	
Close the Mexican border	X	

Majority Position	Conservative	Liberal
Tough immigration laws are necessary/be enforced	X	
Foreign terrorists do not have the rights of American citizens	X	
We should not be involved in Libya		X
Abortion should be legal		X
Death penalty for a murder conviction	X	
Prayer in schools	X	
Religious symbols allowed on government property	X	
Creationism and evolution theory taught in schools	X	
Government money to churches for social services--split	X	X
Oppose same-sex marriage	X	
Totals	**25**	**4**

Table 10: Issues by conservative and liberal ideology

We Are The Majority

For the issues discussed here, the voice of America is solidly conservative. This result will be spun and dismissed by the media as extremist and right-wing fanaticism. They might say the polls are cherry-picked, the issues chosen only for the conservative majority result. Not true. The facts speak volumes.

And remember this: the majority defines what is mainstream, not the media.

Conservatives, We Are The Majority!

Chapter 8

How Did We Get Here?

"The natural progress of things is for liberty to yield and
government to gain ground."[1]

Thomas Jefferson

"There are more instances of abridgment of the freedom of the
people by gradual and silent encroachments of those in power
than by violent and sudden usurpations."[2]

James Madison

We begin to see why only 17% of us believe the government has the consent of the governed. Does our government reflect our conservative views? If the majority of us are conservative, America should have a conservative to moderate government. Instead, we have a liberal to moderate government. Why isn't the majority represented?

The purpose of this book is not to provide an in-depth analysis of how we got here, but instead to provide a wake-up call to Americans. We have to fix this. However, having raised the question, it must be addressed. The ideas briefly covered here are by no means exhaustive or conclusive. They are presented in no particular order. No doubt views will vary widely on which culprit is the most important or if others are the cause.

The Media

Despite advertising to the contrary, most of the media present the progressive, liberal view as mainstream. For example, I read Newsweek for many years until it finally dawned on me that the volume of print given to liberal Democrats was far greater than the print given to conservative Republicans. Also, most of the writers displayed a definite preference for liberal positions. I cancelled my subscription and so did most of America.[*]

---

[*]. Newsweek recently sold for $1 and the buyer took on millions in debt.

Another example is the Fox News Network. Regardless of what you think about the "fair and balanced" motto, Fox News is the most watched cable news network because it is not a forum for strictly liberal positions.

For the weekend of July 16-17, 2011 during primetime, the ratings were:[3]

Network	Number of viewers
Fox	1,050,000
CNN	443,000
MSNBC	441,000

Table 11: Cable news channels by number of viewers

The conservative audience is looking for news viewed from their perspective.

And what does the media tell us about conservative candidates? That conservatives cannot get elected. Every time a conservative candidate shows any momentum, we are blasted by reports of how the candidate must move to the center to have a chance of getting elected. They must have forgotten about Ronald Reagan. Or perhaps they missed this statement by Zogby:

> "There exists a real possibility that making the Republican Party more conservative will expand its base by luring some of the independents into the fold."[4]

The Republican Party seems to buy into the media call for Republican moderates. In the 2008 primaries, Republicans nominated a moderate, not a conservative. The conservative candidate was left in the dust. So was the moderate candidate in the general election. And the media cheered.

Journalists have long maintained that they shape popular opinion and add votes to the candidates of their choice. Maybe this is true, but it's not journalism:

> Journalism: writing characterized by a direct presentation of facts or description of events without an attempt at interpretation.[5]

I guess we could have a spirited discussion whether the media still qualifies as journalists.

The Courts

The court system is in place to administer existing laws and to determine if new laws are constitutional. In section 8 of the Constitution, Powers of *Congress*, we read:

> "To make all Laws which shall be necessary and proper..."
>
> *United States Constitution*

Congress makes the laws. Nowhere in the Constitution is the Judiciary given the task or right to make laws. But today, non-elected judges make law and bypass the people and their elected representatives. In fact, minority positions use the courts for this very reason.

If the majority cannot be swayed, use the court system to impose the position against the will of the people. For example, 7% of our population is atheist, yet 92% of us are often ignored so that the 7% don't feel "uncomfortable" about a religious symbol or reference to God. That is the court system imposing the tyranny of the minority.

Gerrymandering

> Gerrymandering: to divide (a territorial unit) into election districts to give one political party an electoral majority in a large number of districts while concentrating the voting strength of the opposition in as few districts as possible.[5]

Put another way, gerrymandering is a legal way to fix elections. Throughout the U.S., some pretty oddly shaped voting districts exist. Has gerrymandering affected the overall composition of Congress?

The only election that gerrymandering cannot touch is the presidential election. Districts make no difference, just the total vote count per state (and the Electoral College). For the 41 elections held since 1930, we find:[6,7]

	Democrat Majority	Republican Majority
President	55%	45%
Senate	70%	30%
House	76%	24%

Table 12: Presidential and Congressional majorities since 1930

A substantial difference exists between the presidential percentage and the Congressional percentages. The country was almost split on the presidential races, reflecting the national mood between Democrats and Republicans, Conservatives and Liberals. Shouldn't we expect Congress to echo that split? But that is not the case. Democrats are heavily favored. Has gerrymandering weighted Congress against the conservative majority?

Fixing elections by any means should be illegal.

The Candidates

"The aim of every political constitution is, or ought to be, first to obtain for rulers men who possess (the) most wisdom to discern, and most virtue to pursue, the common good of the society;"[8]

James Madison

In the time of our Founding Fathers, public service was a sacrifice. Those chosen for public office were already prominent citizens, either through education or business. They were not professional politicians looking for wealth and power. How far we are from that intent:

82% of us believe our representatives first priority is re-election, not serving the common good of society.[9]

Professional politicians have to get re-elected or they are out of a career. They often have no leadership experience, are not prominent citizens, and make decisions on topics (like economics) that they know nothing about. How reasonable is it to have people making laws about running a business that have never run a business? Or a health care system?

Candidates make promises on who they are and what they will do in office. We vote for them with the hope they will represent our beliefs and values. We are often disappointed. They go against their promises. Scandals abound. Self-interest prevails.

We are all human. We all have faults and weaknesses. But Americans haven't demanded enough of our representatives. We even reward professional politicians for blatantly misrepresenting themselves by re-electing them. We need better candidates, but we will only get them if we demand it and make it clear that they are serving us. If they don't, we must remove them from office.

Term Limits

> "The elective mode of obtaining rulers is the characteristic policy of a republican government. The means relied on in this form of government for preventing their degeneracy are numerous and various. The most effectual one, is such a limitation of the term of appointments as will maintain a proper responsibility to the people."[8]
>
> *James Madison*

Boiling down the language of the 1700's, Madison is saying term limits are the best way to keep a representative focused on the common good of the people. One can infer that Madison would be against professional politicians making a life-long career out of public office.

Unfortunately, the Supreme Court ruled on May 23, 1995 that States cannot impose term limits on their Federal representatives.[10] Nevermind that the representatives are from the States, are elected by the people of the States, and that the States send the representatives to Congress. Nevermind that the states are stripped of a right that the Congress and the States imposed on the presidency with Amendment 22 of the Constitution.

This leaves Congress to impose term limits on themselves. Don't hold your breath. Would term limits act as Madison foresaw and keep representatives focused on the people? It would be worth finding out.

Republican Leadership

Conservatives have been told for decades they must moderate their positions to get elected. The Republican Party leadership, both the party itself and the Congressional leadership, buys into this. The Republican leadership was very uncomfortable with the Tea-Party movement in 2010 and failed to support conservative candidates. Many won anyway. In July of 2011, the same pattern is emerging concerning the 2012 elections.

Either the Republican leadership needs to see that the majority of Americans are conservative, and act accordingly, or voters need to ignore them and do the work required to get their conservative candidates on the ballot. Perhaps the Republican Party would get the message if conservatives stopped sending them money...

Distribution of Government Workers

It stands to reason that those who believe government is a positive force for society will be more attracted to work for the government than those who view government as the problem. Result? A liberal-leaning work force in government. Here are some numbers:

> 75% of registered voters in the District of Columbia are Democrat.[11]

> Only 7% of registered voters in the District of Columbia are Republican.[11]

It is fair to say that more liberals than conservatives live in our nation's capital.

Conservatives are in the odd position of needing their candidate to abhor government as they go to work in the government. Few of us voluntarily choose to work for a company we detest and the percentages above bear this out.

Even when conservatives are elected, the work force of the government is still predominantly liberal, leaving conservatives working against the bulk of the government workers. That cannot be a recipe for conservative success.

Americans Don't Care

Americans don't care. This is a damning statement but:

> Only 56.8% of eligible voters went to the polls in the presidential elections of 2008.[12]

> Mid-term elections from 1974-2006 range from 36.4% to 39.8% of eligible voter turnout.[12] 40.9% for 2010.[13]

Our government affects our economic well-being, our medical care, our retirement, our education system, our national defense, our standing in the world, and so on. Yet a majority of us cannot even go the polls during mid-term elections? It is worth it to again quote Samuel Adams:

> "Let each citizen remember at the moment he is offering his vote...that he is executing one of the most solemn trusts in human society for which he is accountable to God and his country."[14]

Samuel Adams

How can our representatives feel obligated to us, or worry about our consent, if we won't vote? Self-government, which is our republic, requires participation. If we aren't going to participate, we cede our rights to the government. We give our individual rights to the government. Do we care about that?

Chapter 9

Get Out and VOTE

"And what country can preserve its liberties, if its rulers are not
warned from time to time, that this people preserve the spirit
of resistance?"[1]

Thomas Jefferson

"The citizens of the U.S. are responsible for the greatest trust
ever confided to a political society."[2]

James Madison

Conservatives make up the majority of voters in this country. We need a political revolution* that shapes the government to reflect the majority of voters. During the process, the minority will begin to scream "unfair" and that storm must be weathered.

America does not want tyranny by the majority, that is one reason our government is a republic and not a democracy, but tyranny of the minority is just as bad (although that has become acceptable). The check and balances provided by our Constitution will prevent tyranny of the majority, but our system also provides that the make-up of the government should reflect and represent the population.

What To Do

For the conservative majority of this nation, the election of 2010 was a beginning, but only a beginning. We remember the Reagan Revolution, and lament that it didn't last for even the four years following Reagan. We remember the Contract with America in 1994 as Newt Gingrich and the Republicans made loads of promises they didn't keep. We don't want the recent conservative gains in Congress, Governorships, and State legislatures to go the same way. But they will unless the majority unites together for the elections of 2012.

---

*. Peaceful revolution. This is not a call to arms.

The Majority:

- MUST NOT allow the Moderates or Liberals of New Hampshire to choose the Republican presidential candidate

- MUST NOT be fooled by the media coverage of how a conservative candidate must become moderate

- MUST NOT let the politicians and media convince us they know better than we do

- MUST NOT let your hot button issue result in support of a moderate or liberal candidate

- MUST NOT let the media portrayal of conservatives as racist, homophobic, elitist, greedy zealots change your beliefs and values. You are not these things.

And the Majority MUST:

- Determine if your representative represents you. To find out how your representative voted on the issues, go to:

    http://projects.washingtonpost.com/congress/112

    http://www.votesmart.org/index.htm

    http://www.govit.com/government/house

    http://www.govit.com/government/senate

- Take the time and energy to learn the issues and candidates

- Be courageous and vote your beliefs and values

- Forget about being "politically correct" (that is only an attempt to shame you into liberal positions)

- **VOTE** in the primaries for conservative candidates

- **VOTE** in the general election

We Are The Majority!!

References

Chapter 1:

1. Rasmussen Reports (2011, August 7). 17% say the U.S. Government Has the Consent of the Governed. Retrieved from http://www.rasmussenreports.com/public_content/politics/general_politics/august_2011/new_low_17_say_u_s_government_has_consent_of_the_governed

2. Steele, J. Michael, Ph.D (2007, November 14). Polling the Polling Experts: How Accurate and Useful Are Polls These Days? Retrieved from http://knowledge.wharton.upenn.edu/article.cfm?articleid=1843

3. Are Public Opinion Polls Really Accurate? Retrieved from http://thisnation.com/question/002.html

4. Mott, Jonathan, Ph.D. Is the United States a democracy? Retrieved from http://thisnation/question/011.html

5. Madison, James. Federalist Paper Number 10. Retrieved from http://www.founding fathers.info/federalistpapers/fed10.html

6. The Free Dictionary. Retrieved from http//www.freedictionarycom/republic

Chapter 2:

1. Madison, James. (1788, February 19). Federalist Paper Number 57. Retrieved from http://www.founding fathers.info/federalistpapers/fed57.htm

2. Webster's Ninth New Collegiate Dictionary (1985)

3. Adams, Samuel (1781, April 16) Boston Gazette. Retrieved from http://www.heritageofthefoundingfathers.com/quotes.html

4. National Voter Turnout in Federal Elections: 1960-2008. Retrieved from http://www.infoplease.com/ipa/A0781453.html

5. Rasmussen Reports (2011, May 31). Summary of Party Affiliation. Retrieved from http://www.rasmussenreports.com/public_content/archive/mood_of_america_archive/partisan_trends/summary_of_party_affiliation

6. Student News Daily (2010). Conservative vs. Liberal Beliefs. Retrieved from http://www.studentnewsdaily.com/other/conservative-vs-liberal-beliefs

7. Advocates for Self Government (2010). Quiz: What Does Your Score Mean? Retrieved from http://www.theadvocates.org/content/what-does-your-score-mean

8. Messerli, Joe (2011, July 31). Political Ideology Definitions. Retrieved from http://www.balancedpolitics.org/ideology.htm

9. Dictionary.com. Retrieved at http://dictionary.reference.com/browse/moderate

10. Zogby (2009, November 9). The Big Confusion: "Moderates" and "Independents" Are Not the Same Thing. Retrieved from http://www.zogby.com/news/2009/11/09/the-big-confusion-moderates-and-independents-are-not-the-same-thing/

11. Gallup (2010, December 16). Conservatives Continue to Outnumber Moderates in 2010. Retrieved from http://www.gallup.com/poll/145271

Chapter 3:

1. Lincoln, Abraham. Quotes of our Founding Fathers. Retrieved from http://www.dojgov.net/Liberty_Watch.htm

2. Government Spending the United States: Federal State Local 2010. Retrieved from http://www.usgovernmentspending.com/#usgs302a

3. U.S. Census Bureau (2010). Population Distribution and Change: 2000-2010. Retrieved from http://www.census.gov/prod/cen2010/briefs/c2010br-01.pdf

4. Rasmussen Reports (2011, August 7). 17% say the U.S. Government Has the Consent of the Governed. Retrieved from http://www.rasmussenreports.com/public_content/politics/general_politics/august_2011/new_low_17_say_u_s_government_has_consent_of_the_governed

5. Rasmussen Reports (2011, October 24). Congressional Approval. Retrieved from http://www.rasmussenreports.com/public_content/politics/mood_of_america/congressional_performance

6. Rasmussen Reports (2011, June 8). Only 24% Say They Share Obama's Political Views. Retrieved from http://www.rasmussenreports.com/public_content/politics/obama_administration/june_2011/only_24_say_they_share_obama_s_political_views

7. Zogby (2011, April 18). Approval of Republicans in Congress Drops BAck to 31%; One-Point Higher Than That of Democrats. Retrieved from http://www.zogby.com/news/2011/04/18/ibope-zogby-interactive-approval-republicans-congress-drops-back-31-one-point-higher-democrats-/

8. Rasmussen Reports (2010, December 20). Voters Give Mixed Marks to Influence of Religion on Government Policy. Retrieved from http://www.rasmussenreports.com/public_content/politics/general_politics/december_2010/voters_give_mixed_marks_to_influence_of_religion_on_government_policy

9. Ginsberg, Ruth Bader (2010, July 31). Speech given at the International Academy of Comparative Law at American University, entitled "A decent respect to the Opinions of [Human]kind": The Value of a Comparative Perspective in Constitutional Adjudication. Retrieved from http://opiniojuris.org/2010/08/02/justice-ginsburg-on-using-foreign-and-international-law-in-constitutional-adjudication/

10. Zogby (2007, July 2). U.S. Constitution Wearing Well In Modern America. Retrieved from http://zogby.com/news/2007/07/02/zogby-poll-us-constitution-wearing-well-in-modern-america/

11. Rasmussen Reports (2010, November 23). Many Say Government Now Operating Outside the Constitution. Retrieved from http://www.rasmussenreports.com/public_content/politics/general_politics/november_2010/many_say_government_now_operating_outside_the_constitution

12. Constitutional Oath. Retrieved from http://www.supremecourt.gov/about/oath/textoftheoathsofoffice2009.aspx

13. Jefferson, Thomas (1817). Letter to Albert Gallatin. Retrieved from http://econfaculty.gmu.edu/wew/quotes/govt.html

14. Madison, James (1831). Letter to James Robertson. Retrieved from http://en.wikisource.org/wiki/James_Madison_letter_to_James_Robertson

15. Rasmussen Reports (2010, September 7). 68% Favor Smaller Government, Lower Taxes. Retrieved from http://www.rasmussenreports.com/public_content/archive/mood_of_america_archive/benchmarks/68_favor_smaller_government_lower_taxes

16. Rasmussen Reports (2011, June 3). 53% View Government As Threat to Individual Rights. Retrieved from http://www.rasmussenreports.com/public_content/politics/general_politics/may_2011/53_view_government_as_threat_to_individual_rights

Chapter 4:

1. Jefferson, Thomas (1816). Letter to Samuel Kercheval. Retrieved from http://www.freerepublic.com/focus/f-news/2759170/replies?c=5

2. Business Directory. laissez-faire economics. Retrieved from http://www.businessdictionary.com/definition/laissez-faire-economics.html

3. Rasmussen Reports (2011, September 18). 44% Say They're Conservative, 40% Moderate, 11% Liberal on Fiscal Issues,. Retrieved from http://www.rasmussenreports.com/public_content/politics/general_politics/september_2011/44_conservative_40_moderate_11_liberal_on_fiscal_issues

4. What is capitalism? definition and meaning. Retrieved from http://www.investorwords.com/713/capitalism.html

5. What is socialism? definition and meaning. Retrieved from http://www.onvestorwords.com/4613/socialism.html

6. Define Socialism. Retrieved from http://dictionary.reference.com/browse/socialism

7. Define Communism. Retrieved from http://dictionary.reference.com/browse/communism

8. Rasmussen Reports (2011, March 15). 11% Say Communism Better Than U.S. System of Politics and Economics. Retrieved from http://www.rasmussenreports.com/public_content/politics/general_politics/march_2011/11_say_communism_better_than_u_s_system_of_politics_and_economics

9. Capitalism vs. Socialism: Dedatabase-Debate Topics. Retrieved from http://www.idebate.org/debatabase/topic_details.php?topicID=400

10. Marx, Karl & Engels, Friedrich (1848). Manifesto of the Communist Party, Chapter 2. Retrieved from http://www.marxists.org/archive/marx/works/1848/communist-manifesto/ch02.htm

11. Jacobs, Frank (2008, June 16). Federal Lands in the US. Retrieved from http://bigthink.com/ideas/21343

12. Timiraos, Nick (2010, April 30). U.S. Role in Mortgage Market Grows Even Larger. The Wall Street Journal. Retrieved from http://online.wsj.com/article/SB10001424052748704093204575216530213580458.html

13. Rasmussen Reports (2010, April 23). 60% Say Capitalism Better Than Socialism. Retrieved from http://www.rasmussenreports.com/public_content/business/general_business/april_2010/60_say_capitalism_better_than_socialism

14. Gallup (2010, February 4). Socialism Viewed Positively by 36% of Americans. Retrieved from http://www.gallup.com/poll/125645/Socialism-Viewed-Positively-Americans.aspx

15. Jefferson, Thomas (1802, November 29). Letter to Thomas Cooper. Retrieved from http://wiki.monticello.org/mediawiki/index.php/Wasting_the_labours_of_the_people

16. Zogby (2010, March 11). 95% of U.S. Adults Say It's Important to Reduce National Debt, But Are Split On Tax Cuts & Spending to Create Jobs. Retrieved from http://www.zogby.com/news/2010/03/11/zogby-interactive-95-of-us-adults-say-its-important-to-reduce-national-debt-but-are-split-on-tax-cut/

17. Rasmussen Reports (2011, February 17). Voters Think They're Far More Eager To Cut Spending Than Politicians Are. Retrieved from http://www.rasmussenreports.com/public_content/business/general_business/february_2011/voters_think_they_re_far_more_eager_to_cut_spending_than_politicians_are

18. Gallup (2011, April 29). Americans Blame Wasteful Government Spending for Deficit. Retrieved from http://www.gallup.com/poll/147338/Americans-Blame-Wasteful-Government-Spending-Deficit.aspx

19. Gallup (2011, January 26). Americans Oppose Cuts in Education, Social Security, Defense. Retrieved from http://www.gallup.com/poll/145790/Americans-Oppose-Cuts-Education-Social-Security-Defense.aspx

20. Grace Commission Report (1984, January 15). President's Private Sector Survey on cost control. Retrieved from http://www.uhuh.com/taxstuff/gracecom.htm

21. Rasmussen Reports (2011, June 3). Most Voters Still Think Tax Cuts, Spending Decreases Benefit Economy. Retrieved from http://www.rasmussenreports.com/public_content/business/taxes/june_2011/most_voters_still_think_tax_cuts_spending_decreases_benefit_economy

22. Rasmussen Reports (2010, September 7). 68% Favor Smaller Government, Lower Taxes. Retrieved from http://www.rasmussenreports.com/public_content/archive/mood_of_america_archive/benchmarks/68_favor_smaller_government_lower_taxes

23. Madison, James (1794, January 10). Annals of Congress, House of Representatives, 3rd Congress, 1st Session, page 170. Retrieved from http://en.wikiquote.org/wiki/James_Madison

24. Madison, James (1792, March 29). Essay titled Property. Retrieved from http://www.plattecountylandmark.com/Article11398.htm

25. Jefferson, Thomas (1816, April 6). Letter to Joseph Milligan. Retrieved from http://maninthemirror6.wordpress.com/founding-fathers-on-the-redistribution-of-wealth/

26. Franklin, Benjamin (1766, November 29). The London Chronicle article entitled On the Price of Corn, and Management of the Poor. Retrieved from http://www.historycarper.com/resources/twobf3/price.htm

27. Gallup (2011, April 14). Democrats, Republicans Differ Widely on Taxing the Rich. Retrieved from http://www.gallup.com/poll/147104/Democrats-Republicans-Differ-Widely-Taxing-Rich.aspx

28. Obama, Barack (2008, October 12). Talking with plumber Joe Wurzelbacher as reported by ABC News. Retrieved from http://blogs.abcnews.com/politicalpunch/2008/10/spread-the-weal.html

29. Zogby (2010, May 20). 71% Don't Like 'Bank Bailouts,' But Small Majorities See Necessity of Government Intervention. Retrieved from http://www.zogby.com/news/2010/05/20/zogby-interactive-71-dont-like-bank-bailouts-but-small-majorities-see-necessity-of-government-interv/

30. Rasmussen Reports (2011, November 17). 59% Say Bailouts Were Bad For America. Retrieved from http://www.rasmussenreports.com/public_content/business/federal_bailout/november_2011/59_say_government_bailouts_were_bad_for_america

31. Rasmussen Reports (2010, December 10). Americans Still Strongly Favor Audit of the Fed. Retrieved from http://www.rasmussenreports.com/public_content/business/general_business/december_2010/americans_still_strongly_favor_audit_of_the_fed

32. Rasmussen Reports (2011, May 31). 68% Say Bank Bailout Money Went To Those Who Caused Meltdown. Retrieved from http://www.rasmussenreports.com/public_content/business/federal_bailout/may_2011/68_say_bank_bailout_money_went_to_those_who_caused_meltdown

Chapter 5:

1. Jefferson, Thomas (1816, February 2). Letter to Joseph C. Cabell. Retrieved from http://press-pubs.uchicago.edu/founders/documents/v1ch4s34.html

2. Gallup (2009, November 13). More in U.S. Say Health Coverage Is Not Gov't. Responsibility. Retrieved from http://www.gallup.com/poll/124253/Say-Health-Coverage-Not-Gov-Responsibility.aspx

3. Zogby (2010, April 21). 51% of Voters Oppose Healthcare Reform Act. Retrieved from http://www.zogby.com/news/2010/04/21/zogby-interactive-51-of-voters-oppose-healthcare-reform-act/

4. Rasmussen Reports (2011, June 20). Health Care Law. Retrieved from http://www.rasmussenreports.com/public_content/politics/current_events/healthcare/

june_2011/
53_favor_repeal_of_health_care_law_49_say_measure_bad_for_country

5. Gallup (2011, March 16). In U.S., Expanding Energy Output Still Trumps Green Concerns. Retrieved from http://www.gallup.com/poll/146651/Expanding-Energy-Output-Trumps-Green-Concerns.aspx

6. Rasmussen Reports (2010, October 10). Most Voters Still See Finding New Energy Sources As More Important Than Conservation. Retrieved from http://www.rasmussenreports.com/public_content/politics/current_events/environment_energy/
most_voters_still_see_finding_new_energy_sources_as_more_important_than_conservation

7. Snopes.com (2009, September 28). Al Gore's Energy Use. Retrieved from http://www.snopes.com/politics/business/gorehome.asp

8. Zogby (2009, November 19). 52% Say U.S. Has Obligation to Cut Carbon Emissions. Retrieved from http://www.zogby.com/news/2009/11/19/zogby-interactive-52-say-us-has-obligation-to-cut-carbon-emissions/

9. Rasmussen Reports (2009, July 1). 56% Don't Want To Pay More To Fight Global Warming. Retrieved from http://www.rasmussenreports.com/public_content/politics/current_events/environment_energy/
56_don_t_want_to_pay_more_to_fight_global_warming

10. Rasmussen Reports (2011, May 13). 51% Blame Extreme Weather on Long-Term Planetary Trends, 19% Blame Human Activity. Retrieved from http://www.rasmussenreports.com/public_content/politics/current_events/environment_energy/
51_blame_extreme_weather_on_long_term_planetary_trends_19_blame_human_activity

11. Zogby (2011, June 8). Nature's Wrath? Most Say Cycles, Not Climate Change to Blame. Retrieved from http://www.zogby.com/news/2011/06/08/ibope-zogby-poll-natures-wrath-most-say-cycles-not-climate-change-to-blame/

12. Pew Research (2011, June 10). Views of Middle East Unchanged by Recent Events. Retrieved from http://pewresearch.org/pubs/2020/poll-american-attitudes-foreign-policy-middle-east-israel-palestine-obama

13. Rasmussen Reports (2011, April 15). 42% Favor More U.S. Nuclear Power Plants. Retrieved from http://www.rasmussenreports.com/public_content/politics/current_events/environment_energy/
42_favor_more_u_s_nuclear_power_plants

14. Gallup (2010, March 22). U.S. Support for Nuclear Power Climbs to New High of 62%. Retrieved from http://www.gallup.com/poll/126827/Support-Nuclear-Power-Climbs-New-High.aspx

15. Obama, Barack (2008, January 17). Quoted in an interview with the San Francisco Chronicle. Retrieved from http://www.sfgate.com/cgi-bin/blogs/opinionshop/detail?entry_id=23562

16. Gallup (2010, July 27). Amid Immigration Debate, Americans' Views Ease Slightly. Retrieved from http://www.gallup.com/poll/141560/Amid-Immigration-Debate-Americans-Views-Ease-Slightly.aspx

17. Rasmussen Reports (2011, June 1). 65% Say Those Who Hire Illegal Immigrants Bigger Problem Than Immigrants Themselves (which references the 2008 study quoted here). Retrieved from http://www.rasmussenreports.com/public_content/politics/current_events/immigration/65_say_those_who_hire_illegal_immigrants_bigger_problem_than_immigrants_themselves

18. Gallup (2010, July 6). Americans Closely Divided Over Immigration Reform Priority. Retrieved from http://www.gallup.com/poll/141113/Americans-Closely-Divided-Immigration-Reform-Priority.aspx

19. Gallup (2010, May 4). Americans Value Both Aspects of Immigration Reform. Retrieved from http://www.gallup.com/poll/127649/Americans-Value-Aspects-Immigration-Reform.aspx

20. Zogby (2010, April 28). Large Majority Opposes Equal Right for Illegal Immigrants, But Support Human Rights Protection. Retrieved from http://www.zogby.com/news/2010/04/28/zogby-interactive-large-majority-opposes-equal-rights-for-illegal-immigrants-but-support-human-right/

21. Rasmussen Reports (2011, November 18). New High: 65% Oppose Automatic Citizenship for Children Born Here to Illegal Immigrants. Retrieved from http://www.rasmussenreports.com/public_content/politics/current_events/immigration/new_high_65_oppose_automatic_citizenship_for_children_born_here_to_illegal_immigrants

22. Rasmussen Reports (2011, June 11). 58% Want English-Only Ballots. Retrieved from http://www.rasmussenreports.com/public_content/politics/general_politics/june_2011/58_want_english_only_ballots

23. Obama, Barack (2008, July 8). Campaign speech in Powder Springs, GA. Retrieved from http://online.worldmag.com/2008/07/09/obama-make-sure-your-child-can-speak-spanish/

24. Gallup (2010, July 9). Americans Oppose Federal Suit Against Ariz. Immigration Law. Retrieved from http://www.gallup.com/poll/141209/Americans-Oppose-Federal-Suit-Against-Ariz-Immigration-Law.aspx

25. Rasmussen Reports (2011, March 14). Most Voters Still Support Guantanamo Prison, Military Tribunals for Terrorists. Retrieved from http://www.rasmussenreports.com/public_content/politics/general_politics/march_2011/most_voters_still_support_guantanamo_prison_military_tribunals_for_terrorists

26. Adams, John & Jefferson, Thomas (1786, March 28). Letter to John Jay. Retrieved from http://cojs.org/cojswiki/Thomas_Jefferson_to_John_Jay,_1786.

27. Rasmussen Reports (2011, February 8). 27% See UN As U.S. Ally, 15% As An Enemy. Retrieved from http://www.rasmussenreports.com/public_content/politics/general_politics/february_2011/27_see_un_as_u_s_ally_15_as_an_enemy

28. Gallup (2011, February 28). Americans Maintain Broad Support for Israel. Retrieved from http://www.gallup.com/poll/146408/Americans-Maintain-Broad-Support-Israel.aspx

29. Rasmussen Reports (2011, April 23). Voters Remain Closely Divided Over Libya. Retrieved from http://www.rasmussenreports.com/public_content/politics/general_politics/april_2011/voters_remain_closely_divided_over_libya

30. Zogby (2011, March 29). Most Fear Future Quagmire in Libya. Retrieved from http://www.zogby.com/news/2011/03/29/zogby-interactive-most-fear-future-quagmire-in-libya/

31. Madison, James (1794, January 10). Speech in the House of Representatives. Retrieved from http://www.revolutionary-war-and-beyond.com/james-madison-quotes-7.html

32. Jefferson, Thomas (1821, August 18). Letter to Charles Hammond. Retrieved from http://www.revolutionary-war-and-beyond.com/quotes-by-thomas-jefferson.html

33. Rasmussen Reports (2010, March 23). 49% Support State Lawsuits Against Health Care Plan. Retrieved from http://www.rasmussenreports.com/public_content/politics/current_events/healthcare/march_2010/49_support_state_lawsuits_against_health_care_plan

34. Zogby (2011, February 22). Majorities Say States Can Cut Employee Salaries & Void Collective Bargaining Agreements. Retrieved from http://www.zogby.com/news/2011/02/22/zogby-interactive-majorities-say-states-can-cut-employee-salaries-void-collective-bargaining-agreeme/

35. Gallup (2011, March 9). Americans' Message to States: Cut, Don't Tax and Borrow. Retrieved from http://www.gallup.com/poll/146525/Americans-Message-States-Cut-Dont-Tax-Borrow.aspx

Chapter 6:

1. Jefferson, Thomas (1782). Notes on the State of Virginia, Query XVIII. Retrieved from http://en.wikiquote.org/wiki/Thomas_Jefferson

2. Gallup (2011, June 3). More Than 9 in 10 Americans Continue to Believe in God. Retrieved from http://www.gallup.com/poll/147887/Americans-Continue-Believe-God.aspx

3. Adams, John (1787). The Works of John Adams, 6:9, p. 280. Retrieved from http://www.ourrepubliconline.com/OurRepublic/Topic/39

4. Washington, George (1789, April 30). First Inaugural Address. Retrieved from http://www.archives.gov/legislative/features/gw-inauguration/

5. Adams, John (1798, October 11). Letter to the Officers of the First Brigade of the Third Division of the Militia of Massachusetts. Retrieved from http://www.beliefnet.com/resourcelib/docs/115/Message_from_John_Adams_to_the_Officers_of_the_First_Brigade_1.html

6. Pew Forum (2010). Church Statistics and Religious Affiliations. Retrieved from http://religions.pewforum.org/affiliations

7. Rasmussen Reports (2010, April 25). 80% Say Religious Faith is Important To Their Daily Lives. Retrieved from http://www.rasmussenreports.com/public_content/lifestyle/general_lifestyle/april_2010/80_say_religious_faith_is_important_to_their_daily_lives

8. Pew Forum (2006, August 24). Many Americans Uneasy with Mix of Religion and Politics. Retrieved from http://pewforum.org/Politics-and-Elections/Many-Americans-Uneasy-with-Mix-of-Religion-and-Politics.aspx

9. Pew Forum (2009, October 1). Support for Abortion Slips. Retrieved from http://pewforum.org/Abortion/Support-for-Abortion-Slips.aspx

10. Pew Forum (2007, December 19). An Enduring Majority: Americans Continue to Support the Death Penalty. Retrieved from http://pewforum.org/Death-Penalty/An-Enduring-Majority-Americans-Continue-to-Support-the-Death-Penalty.aspx

11. Rasmussen Reports (2011, February 11). 65% of Americans Favor Prayer in Public Schools. Retrieved from http://www.rasmussenreports.com/public_content/lifestyle/general_lifestyle/february_2011/65_of_americans_favor_prayer_in_public_schools

12. Pew Forum (2007, May 9). Religion in the Public Schools. Retrieved from http://pewforum.org/Church-State-Law/Religion-in-the-Public-Schools%284%29.aspx

13. Rasmussen Reports (2010, December 13). Americans Still Favor Religious Symbols on Public Land, Religious Holidays in the Schools. Retrieved from http://www.rasmussenreports.com/public_content/lifestyle/holidays/december_2010/americans_still_favor_religious_symbols_on_public_land_religious_holidays_in_the_schools

14. Pew Forum (2007, June 27). Religious Displays and the Courts. Retrieved from http://pewforum.org/Church-State-Law/Religious-Displays-and-the-Courts.aspx

15. Pew Forum (2005, August 30). Public Divided on Origins of Life. Retrieved from http://pewforum.org/Politics-and-Elections/Public-Divided-on-Origins-of-Life.aspx

16. Pew Forum (2009, November 16). Faith-Based Programs Still Popular, Less Visible. Retrieved from http://pewforum.org/Social-Welfare/Faith-Based-Programs-Still-Popular-Less-Visible.aspx

17. Pew Forum (2009, July 9). A Contentious Debate: Same-Sex Marriage in the U.S. Retrieved from http://pewforum.org/Gay-Marriage-and-Homosexuality/A-Contentious-Debate-Same-Sex-Marriage-in-the-US.aspx

Chapter 7:

1. Hamilton, Alexander (1787, December 14). Federalist Paper Number 22. Retrieved from http://www.foundingfathers.info/federalistpapers/fed22.htm

Chapter 8:

1. Jefferson, Thomas (1788, May 27). Letter to Edward Carrington. Retrieved from http://www.monticello.org/site/jefferson/natural-progress-things-quotation

2. Madison, James (1788, June 6). Speech at the Virginia Convention to ratify the Federal Constitution. Retrieved from http://en.wikiquote.org/wiki/James_Madison

3. Cable News Ratings for Saturday-Sunday, July 16-17, 2011. Retrieved from http://tvbythenumbers.zap2it.com/2011/07/19/cable-news-ratings-for-saturday-sunday-july-16-17-2011/98312/

4. Zogby (2009, November 9). The Big Confusion: "Moderates" and "Independents" Are Not the Same Thing. Retrieved from http://

www.zogby.com/news/2009/11/09/the-big-confusion-moderates-and-independents-are-not-the-same-thing/

5. Webster's Ninth New Collegiate Dictionary (1985)

6. List of Presidents of the United States. Retrieved from http://en.wikipedia.org/wiki/List_of_Presidents_of_the_United_States

7. Composition of Congress, by Political Party, 1855-2010. Retrieved from http://www.infoplease.com/ipa/A0834721.html

8. Madison, James (1788, February 19). Federalist Paper Number 57. Retrieved from http://www.foundingfathers.info/federalistpapers/fed57.htm

9. Rasmussen Reports (2010, December 20). Voters Give Mixed Marks to Influence of Religion on Government Policy. Retrieved from http://www.rasmussenreports.com/public_content/politics/general_politics/december_2010/voters_give_mixed_marks_to_influence_of_religion_on_government_policy

10. U.S. Supreme Court (1995, May 23). U.S. Term Limits, Inc. v. Thornton. Retrieved from http://en.wikipedia.org/wiki/U.S._Term_Limits,_Inc._v._Thornton

11. District of Columbia Democratic State Committee. Retrieved from http://en.wikipedia.org/wiki/District_of_Columbia_Democratic_State_Committee

12. National Voter Turnout in Federal Election: 1960-2008. Retrieved from http://www.infoplease.com/iap/A0781453.html

13. 2010 General Election Turnout Rates (2011, January 28). Retrieved from http://elections.gmu.edu/Turnout_2010G.html

14. Adams, Samuel (1781, April 16) Boston Gazette. Retrieved from http://www.heritageofthefoundingfathers.com/quotes.html

Chapter 9:

1. Jefferson, Thomas (1787, November 13). Letter to William S. Smith. Retrieved from http://en.wikiquote.org/wiki/Rebellion

2. Madison, James. Address to the States. The Mind of the Founder: Sources of the Political Thought of James Madison, (New York: The Bobbs-Merrill Company, Inc., 1973), p. 32.

List of Tables

About the Author

Scott is a fledging technical writer, recently making a mid-life career change. While the change was somewhat forced upon him by the economic downturn in 2008, he considers it a blessing.

He also writes Christian fiction.

And, he is blessed with a loving wife, four wonderful children, and three lovely grandchildren (so far). He lives in the bustling Atlanta area and, as of this writing, so do the rest of his family.

About the Author

www.ingramcontent.com/pod-product-compliance
Lightning Source LLC
Chambersburg PA
CBHW022123280326
41933CB00007B/515